In the Metro

University of Minnesota Press

Minneapolis · London

In the Metro

Marc Augé

Translated

and with an

Introduction

and

Afterword

by

Tom Conley

The University of Minnesota Press gratefully acknowledges financial assistance for the translation of this book provided by the French Ministry of Culture—Centre national du livre.

The University of Minnesota Press appreciates the expert work of David Thorstad on the translation of this book.

The map of the Paris metro has been reproduced here courtesy of the R.A.T.P.

Photographs copyright 2002 Mark Neumann

Originally published as *Un ethnologue dans le métro*, copyright Hachette, 1986.

Published by the University of Minnesota Press
111 Third Avenue South, Suite 290
Minneapolis, MN 55401-2520
http://www.upress.umn.edu

Library of Congress Cataloging-in-Publication Data

Augé, Marc.
    [Ethnologue dans le métro. English]
    In the metro / Marc Augé ; translated and with an introduction and afterword by Tom Conley.
        p.   cm.
    Includes bibliographical references.
    ISBN 0-8166-3436-X (hc.) — ISBN 0-8166-3437-8 (pbk.)
    1. Ethnology—Philosophy.   I. Title.
    GN345 .A9213 2002

                                        2002002330
Printed in the United States of America on acid-free paper

The University of Minnesota is an equal-opportunity educator and employer.

12 11 10 09 08 07 06 05 04 03 02   10 9 8 7 6 5 4 3 2 1

Contents

Introduction: Marc Augé, "A Little History"
Tom Conley

For years the tall and slender Michelin Green Guide, a treasure trove of information and savvy for every tourist, has offered words about the background of notable monuments and places under a rubric titled "Un peu d'histoire." A little history might be useful in helping us to situate and to discern how Marc Augé, a veteran anthropologist of cultures in the southern regions of the Ivory Coast, came to write *In the Metro*, a book that defies classification as a work either of ethnography or of literature. The Proustian tenor of an account of an anthropologist's descent into the tunnels of rapid transit has few models for comparison.[1] The contours of the reflective travelogue stand to gain sharper lines when they are set in contrast to Augé's professional work. "A little history" can also serve as an emblem of a shift in the mode of inquiry that Augé heralded when he wrote his studies of African culture with the aim of bringing together the virtues of structural method and the colonial history of Africa. His departure from the anthropological canon may also be a return to and a revision of some of its guiding principles.

In the context of the paragraphs that follow, "a little history" cannot risk being so dangerous as "a little knowledge." The lines of the writer's background tie the recent studies of the ethnographer as tourist to the khaki-clad ethnologist living in the midst of traditional cultures, but also, as we shall discover, to the ethnologist as an engaged theorist of political science.[2] It might also—and such is the aim of this Introduction—serve to locate some parallels between the early and later writings of an ethnographer who has emerged over the past decade less as an accomplished student of traditional societies than as a French writer of the first order. That Augé inspires his public through a style of inquiry is an attested fact; that his work invites us to broaden the field of his investigations and to follow similar lines of reflection on our own shall be the topic taken up in the Afterword appended to this translation.

Marc Augé belongs, he avows, to a generation of ethnologists trained in the 1960s. The moment was felicitous. The impact of a tradition of indelibly French signature, known through the kinship of Émile Durkheim and Marcel Mauss, had been recently confirmed in the model work and inspired teaching of Claude Lévi-Strauss. The successive publication of his *Structures élémentaires de la parenté* (1949), *Tristes Tropiques* (1955), *Anthropologie structurale* (1958), and *La Pensée sauvage* (1962), prior to *Le Cru et le cuit* (1964), the first volume of his Homeric *Mythologiques* (final volume appearing in 1971), bore witness to the ascendancy of structuralism. By virtue of its principles, notes Augé in one of the many elusive autobiographical flickers in his own copious oeuvre, the new mode of thought was summoning a functionalist vision of culture.[3] Questioned at the time was the belief, first, in final causes adhering to the view that cultures have discernible and cohering traits that might be called *"philoso-*

phies" or "beliefs." Interrogated second was the mechanistic aspect of Marxian claims to the effect that the sum of values defining a given culture can be attributed to an economic infra-structure.[4] In place of these views and heralded in the work of Lévi-Strauss, Cornelius Castoriadis, and Louis Althusser was a new relation with the *other*. After seeing how these ethnographers were equating the latter with the unknown, the bedrock of life itself, Augé noted that the same pioneers were running the risk of reducing the social "actualization of the self's relations to others" to a religion of mystery and unfounded exoticism. Without going so far as Jacques Derrida, who had recently called Lévi-Strauss the proponent of an inverted ethnocentrism, Augé claimed that the relation with the unknown was liable to being reified or idolized at a time when globalization was extinguishing the allure of remote peoples and places.[5] Evidence was clear. Shortly after 1968, oceanic passage by boat was curtailed: two luxury liners, the *France* and the *United States,* were packed in mothballs; transoceanic air travel became a mean; use of satellites for electronic communication caused the world to shrink at a logarithmic progression; in the population explosion all over the world, the other was all of a sudden not only accessible and omnipresent but also pullulating.

In this context that marked the mid-1960s, at the age of twenty-five, Augé put his splendid scholarly training to work by making the first of many trips to and from the Alladian cultures situated along a lagoon stretching to the west of Abidjan on the southern shore of the Ivory Coast. Traveling by air, then by dugout canoe, and at times with a Land Rover, he reached his destinations. There resulted from a sojourn between November 1965 and May 1967 a brilliant monograph, *Le Rivage alladian: Organisation et évolution des villages alladian.*[6] The introduction begins with what he calls "the impressions of a tourist" before giving way to more delicate issues concerning method and style of observation. Contrary to classical studies that had sought to typify the defining traits of a culture without history or writing, he built the research on three bases. The first was in fact the history of the Alladian country before and in the midst of its colonization under white rule, especially since 1840; the second entailed study of familial and matrimonial structures in terms of physical space, along with economic factors (influx of captives bought and sold, trade of ivory, gold, rubber, wood, and ultimately palm oil); the third, which becomes an enduring theme in Augé's work in general, was devoted to spiritual power, to *awa*, an ambiguous force belonging to witches and sorcerers. The latter, he argued, is crucial to the culture and its vicissitudes. The *awabo*, those who embody the malefic power, seemed to him to "constitute a society that seems at once to be the inverse and the double of the 'normal' society" (14). *Awa* and its users were involved in negotiations of the lagoon society with Christian and colonial influences. In examining how the Alladians were mediating the impact of white societies, Augé was following the lead of one of his teachers, Georges Balandier, an Africanist who had been among the first generation of political anthropologists to study the effect of colonization (and that of ethnologists) on the myriad cultures of black Africa.

As a result, the texture of the picture he paints of the Alladian cultures is moving and almost cinematographic. It takes up geography and its relation to economy, but also economy in both material and spiritual manifestations. Augé is impelled to call social formation a series of moving variables that includes kinship, economy, politics, and religion. In these "different rhythms of evolution" that run through "the permanence of a language that outlives changes in structure and the diverse solicitations of history" (245) are found "correspondences" (a word to which we shall return) that define Alladian identity through ties of family, locale, and a sense of enterprise. Power, related to prestige, is also defined by the fears it carries for both its bearers and those on whom it is exerted.

The reader of *Le Rivage alladian* senses that Augé appeals to the codes of the anthropological *monograph* (a theme he will take up in *In the Metro*) when pondering whether an urban ethnography can still be written in the style that students of the discipline learned to master early in their careers in the postwar years. A different impression is gained from a sequel, *Théorie des pouvoirs et idéologie: Étude de cas en Côte d'Ivoire*,[7] a long "case study" of the same cultures that is written at once far from and yet under the shadow of the "events" of May 1968.[8] Three successive trips to the Alladian Lagoon (one for the duration of a year, between April 1968 and April 1969; another from the end of 1969 to the end of January 1970; and the summer of 1971, all of which were subsidized by the Centre National de Recherche Scientifique) allowed Augé to extend his work to the Avikan and Ebrié areas on the same narrow stretch of land. *Théorie des pouvoirs et idéologie* studied in detail the networks of power in Alladian culture, especially in light of the effect of a black Christian prophet, Albert Atcho, who was changing some of the traditional modes of the interrogation of cadavers, the confessions of sorcerers, and exhortations to the community in ways that were directing established practices in the culture toward both colonial and seemingly indigenous ends. The image that inaugurates the study is telling in the oblique way the *incipit* bears a date that cannot fail to infer the aftermath of the events of May in Paris:

November 1968. The rainy season was not yet over, and on that very night lightning bolts, silent flashes of distant thunderclaps, were zigzagging across the sky.

At Bregbo the flickering halos of the storm lamps were multiplying in the depth of the streets and the courtyards. Conversation was abuzz. For this evening the ultimate whispers were not yet heard when, set outside as a night-light, the lamp was nothing more than the reassuring guardian for insomniacs, the sighting point for the vagabonds of dream who every night escape the narrow and vacillating circle in which the mysteries of the night are conjured. This evening, festival reigned. A good deal of the village was going to Albert Atcho's place to wait and listen: the devils having come from a village on the coast, confused by the accusation of a dead person and the avowals of his assassin, were going to appear before the prophet to confess their wrongs and to account for their crimes. (xiii)

Thus the case study is staged. It proceeds to show how social inequalities in the societies built on kinship relations mesh with and find themselves exploited by new—white—modes of domination felt not only under the creeping sprawl of Abidjan, but also in an alluring and strange mix of religious practices.

The result on Augé's part is an ideological anthropology that uses study of religion and economy to adumbrate and refine Marxian and Althusserian models current in Paris at the same time. Augé coins the substantive *ideo-logic,* what he calls the shifting and multilayered logic of "imaginary relations to real modes of production," to consider issues of cultural transference from both economic and psychoanalytic angles. Taken up are representations of the world, representations of the person in view of a theory of sorcery, and those mixing political and religious convictions. The sum of their representations, he advanced, needed to be seen in "their relation with socioeconomic structures." *Ideo-logic* deals with the "logical sum of the representations of a given society."[9] Through the study of ways that a subject can believe in sorcery Augé gathers a sense of the ideology of power as well as the elements that justify it and allow it to be transmitted and reproduced. A tessellation of representations is seen in the relations among overlapping discourses from different sectors of Alladian life.

"Problematic here is the nature of these relations," especially once there is observed "the logical simultaneity, on the one hand, of notions of organization and representation and, on the other, of different types of organization," such that their *syntax,* their ordering or spacing, becomes a paramount concern. At stake is, "in this sense, the syntax of the theoretical discourse of the society cast upon itself" (xix), and all the more when it cannot be named or reduced to a summary configuration or a schematic definition. He notes that in both Atcho's theater and the work of earlier Bregbo prophets, various silences and gaps in speech and performance become symptoms of the relations of individuals to their own symbolic process, community, and the alterities they cultivate.

A cornerstone in *Théorie des pouvoirs et idéologie* is the critique of any anthropology that carries the holistic ambition of explaining a culture by a "philosophy" or a set of conscious beliefs. The exemplary work of this kind in African studies had been *La Philosophie bantoue* by Reverend Father Tempels, a monograph that Augé excoriates by noting that it is impossible for any ethnologist to set in place a closed system that reduces thought to consciousness without taking heed of the ambivalences that riddle all psychic and social life. He counters with *ideo-logic,* a concept that "is not a philosophy even insofar as it is not offered as a continuous and closed discourse on man and the world. It is defined inversely as the unformulated system to which each of the many theories among lagoon societies that can be reproduced owes its own coherence and its relation to other theories—all theories recouping but not being superimposed upon each other, each of them liable to be called forth and used in given circumstances that do not necessarily appeal to other ends" (120–21). Symbolic process is thus perpetual, changing according to contingent forces, but also a function of structures that it needs to represent in order to make itself felt. In his fieldwork on ritual confession, Augé finds the keys to the transmutations of interrelated systems of kinship and power. A subtle and practical model of ideology runs against those that had risked replacing functional paradigms with mystificatory or patently dialectical views of the social process.

Where a philosophy or a "vision of the world" would be a commodity for consumers of nineteenth-century novels or of exotic fiction, Augé's concept of *ideo-logic* affords the "individual" a place whence he or she can scrutinize the effects of alienation that mark consciousness in general. Paris of 1968 (rife with debates about ideology and its types of apparatus) and the

Alladian shores (seen in light of two centuries of colonial history) are thus implicitly juxtaposed and endowed with comparative virtue. So, in order to discern what might be the nature of Alladian alienation—over and above any philosophy or system of belief—Augé posits a kind of existential territorialization to define life along the lagoon. Individuals in the system of lineage and power are compelled at any moment to "take stock of themselves, to situate their place and measure their possible displacements in respect to the sum of worlds that surround them" (130). It follows that Alladian life resembles a condition of doubt, "a perpetual interrogation" about what life is, "an incessant effort to decrypt from everyday reality the ambiguous traces of surreality whence it issues and that alone make life meaningful" (136). For the Alladian, life is lived according to good (but not necessarily common) sense, but everything that gives it significance—birth, love, marriage, childbearing, death—defies reason. An originary madness of being, if a literary trope can be borrowed from the idiolect of Maurice Blanchot, informs the ritual scene on which *Théorie des pouvoirs et idéologie* is based. A *non-sens* at the crux of all meaning seems to be the keystone of the theory, at least if we interpret the "satisfaction" that the person he describes as "a sociologist of culture" gains when he or she can incorporate its inherent alterities into a program of research. The last sentence of the book reads thus: "And so the satisfaction that the sociologist can retain from the possibly illusory feeling of understanding a history of the present is doubled by a more bitter *prise de conscience*: at its conclusion, his or her reflection merely formulates a pessimistic interrogation of the meaning of a *non-sens*" (420).

The psychoanalytic cast of this view of the Alladians in their world betrays well the political dimension of Augé's ethnology. He notes that for the subject in these societies, any "theory" or explicit philosophy would necessarily, because of the ties of lineage to the logic of representation in the theater of public confession, remain in silence. The mere thought of such a theory "reveals the dangers of the capture of speech, it threatens to condemn those who would be impudent enough to take recourse to it in order to develop a clearly stated discourse, a clearly formulated accusation" (226). The point is congruent with what Michel de Certeau saw in 1968 in the rain and ashes flowing down the gutters of Paris in the season of autumnal storms. In the opening pages of *The Capture of Speech* Certeau showed that when the protests by students in early May were buttressed by the revolt of workers later in the same month, and that when the nation soon went on strike for a duration of forty-four days, a population was stating something it could not quite put in words about contradiction and alienation. Whatever discourse there was could only be recuperated by the owners of power. No adequate lexicon was available to articulate the plight other than in the floating syntax of *métro, boulot, dodo* (an issue that Augé will address elegantly and with timeliness in the last sentences of *In the Metro*). The vocabularies of Marxist prophets or of lifelong affiliates of the French Communist Party were, if not dinosauric, completely out of context. There was no way to describe a need for which adequate words existed without them being immediately co-opted and turned against their utterers.

Augé found a nagging expression of similar dilemmas in the reception of Christian inflections of Bregbo rituals. Albert Atcho adroitly turned a fairly traditional concept of sin toward a colonial end. For Bregbo preachers, every individual had been at the origin of his or her own misfortune, but in a milieu belonging less to the self than to the complexities of the social sphere. In the new regime, misfortune was turned into a drama of totally individual failure (277–78). Each penitent became "free" and was "liberated" from the constraints of the symbolic process that had assured tribal solidarity. The inhabitants of the Ebrié Lagoon were slowly dispossessed both of their lands and of themselves. Imposition of plantations and tourism left the population in a *solitude of liberty.* "More than ever, now the Ebrié are condemned to see in the Ivorian forces of modernization the sign of their failure and their exclusion, their vital space being shrunk like a wild ass's skin; for many, they are condemned in some way to an immobile emigration: urbanized without having left their village but nonetheless in having lost it irremediably."[10]

Solitude of liberty in the individual, on the one hand, and, on the other, destruction of life and symbolic process in the communities: the model of *ideo-logic* accounts for the changes in Alladian life not through an account of takeover or of unilateral power relations, nor quite even of a dialectic of master and slave, but rather through a more perniciously dialogic process. Augé detects it in the rupture of lineage through gently negotiated shifts in ritual behavior. The pattern can be discerned, perhaps, through the history of neo-existential labors that in 1968 Félix Guattari would call "existential reterritorialization" and that would apply to the making of fourth-world populations in the first world. In every event, Augé's take on recent Alladian history remains a subtle assessment of a process that Jean Comaroff and John Comaroff discovered in British relations with South Africa over the past two centuries, which the authors summarize in broad strokes: "The essence of colonization inheres less in political overrule than in seizing and transforming 'others' by the very act of conceptualizing, inscribing, and interacting with them on terms not of their choosing; in making them into the pliant objects and silent subjects of our scripts and scenarios; in assuming the capacity to 'represent' them, the active verb itself conflating politics and poetics."[11]

Thus are the Alladians "freed" and "liberated" from their structures of kinship and their lands where they continue to live. In ruminating on the sad condition of things he observes between 1968 and 1970, Augé wonders if the radical politics in Paris of the same years might have correlative worth. Gilles Deleuze and Félix Guattari were not far from his mind. Their attempt to "dissolve" the self or the autonomous "ego" (what now goes by "moi-je" [me-I] in oral expression in contemporary France) into affiliation with "groupuscular" units that move and interact with each other, he noted, might be reflective of a countermovement that would strengthen and shift in different ways some of the patterns of lineage frayed by ritual process in the service of colonial ends.[12] The drive to "dissolve the self" runs counter to Atcho's wish to impose self-identity upon the indigenous mind-set. Yet some sort of "self" is required, Augé follows, if groupuscular counteridentities can be formulated. Any individual would need to take close account of the ideologies at play in the shifting representations assigned to confer meaning upon Alladian culture. The end of the long study implicitly returns to the inaugural image of the storm lamps illuminating the festive and Baroque decor in which Albert Atcho performs a public confession of the devils of the village. When they cope with the accusations leveled against them by a cadaver and the avowals of its assassin, or when they recognize the *non-sens* of their being, they are rewarded with the freedom of isolation and solitude.

The work on lagoon culture determines much of Augé's later writings. At least four elements appear to be transported to and from the Ivory Coast and Paris. First and foremost is the observation that solitude accrues as the world accelerates. Where greater access to technologies of "communication" is obtained, a greater degree of isolation results. (It suffices to look at pedestrians using portable telephones—less in subways than above ground—who seem to be isolating themselves in the streets their feet are touching and from the people who pace before their eyes in order not to talk with an interlocutor but to show the ambient world that their narcissistic plenitude can last as long as they have numbers to dial.) The solitude of which he writes in his studies of daily life in the subway or airports has its bearings in the nefarious effects observed in Bregbo and Ebrié.

A second element is that the dialogue of the "self and the other" is anchored in at least two areas. One, of course, is the ambivalent process found in the variously collective and plural self in Alladian culture. It is found in Paris, the filmgoer's capital of the world, in those fugacious moments when the spectator recognizes in the actors on the screen "the existence of an Other (the author) analogous to himself or herself, analogous to the I-subject of perception."[13] It is a rare instance, inverse to the

Lacanian mirror stage, in which *l'Autre est un Je,* in which the classic Rimbaldian formula of surreality and *non-sens* is turned to mean that "the other is an I." It is best felt in the subway: the anthropologist sees among riders in the subway who stare at the masses in their midst, like himself, a plethora of others-who-are-I's. These persons seem to be looking for a subterranean community. For Augé its absence is sensed in a Proustian way as a deception or disillusionment that is imperiously vital for social consciousness. The beginnings of the dynamics that were studied in religious ritual are transported into the observations of life in a context where most modes of ethnographic inquiry would appear to be out of place.

A third element is the *non-lieu* or "nonplace" and, as corollary, the shrinkage of space that marks postcolonial culture. The nonplace is an ambiguous site in which a person experiences a mix of pleasure and uneasiness of self-suspension. It is the waiting room beyond the security gate of an airport: the passenger consigns himself or herself to living in attendant expectation of an event that will take place when the boarding of the craft is announced; it is perpetuated in the anticipation of calm when we find our seat in the plane but is dashed when the constraints of space remind us that we are human cattle; the pleasure recurs in the wait for the drink and food that will help to consume and pass the time, but the deception returns with the tastelessness of the fare. In the context of Augé's writing, the nonplace bears resemblance to Deleuze's *lieu quelconque* or "any-place-whatsoever" in that the world in which we move is evacuated of alterity and difference.[14] Augé finds it in the erasure of a myriad sense of place that had been part of the mentality and the social geography to the west of Abidjan in the late 1960s, in the growing "migrations toward the city, new populations, and the extension of industrial cultures."[15] The ethnographer's phantasm of an originary and perpetual "place" of habitation, a place nourished with meaning, would serve the desire to construct closed and self-contained worlds, like functional philosophies, outside of "ideo-logical" process. Return to the city enables the illusion to be studied as just that, when mental and physical compression are the pertinent traits of the new urban experience.

Fourth, oblivion and aberration of memory are what Augé might be putting forward as a constructive antidote to the condition of solitude. In the loss of memory is assured the drive to go ahead and to return to anodyne places in order that they can be transformed into vital spaces. In *Les Formes de l'oubli*,[16] Augé revisits the world of literature, of Proust and Julien Gracq in particular, to argue for our "duty to forget." With it "comes vigilance, inquiry, and the actualization of memory in order that we can imagine in the present what might resemble the past" (120). In no other place does Augé underscore so well a convergence of the tasks of the writer of literature and those of the ethnographer. We should recall that *In the Metro* begins under the rubric of "memories" before giving way to "solitudes" and, in a sort of apotheosis of things past and present, in "correspondences" that link souvenir to isolation. A reader of Augé's oeuvre in general senses that the process of writing itself brings forward and establishes memory, and that the "track" or "line" of its reason casts mental images aside. Memory is elided as the work moves forward.

In his years as director of seminars at the École des Hautes Études en Sciences Sociales in Paris, for some time before his recent retirement, Augé shifted from circumscribed research on African cultures to consideration of the status of anthropology in the world at large. The crisis of the discipline and the need to hold to its modes of inquiry are the topic of *A Sense of the Other*. These modes are practiced in theoretical fashion in *Non-lieux* and *La Guerre des rêves,* and so also in some delightful reflections on the movement between urban and country residences in *Domaines et châteaux*.[17] They are put to work in a deceptively powerful preface to a rich volume of photographs documenting the 1930s in Paris.[18] In *Paris années trente: Roger-Viollet* Augé culls through panoplies of black-and-white images in the collection of the Documentation Générale Photographique

Roger-Viollet established by Henri Roger and his spouse, Jeanne Viollet. We observe them across the abyss of the Second World War. In musing on the photographs—on how our hindsight can barely grasp the existential situations of masses in the toss of news about the Spanish civil war, about the Popular Front, fascism, the ultraright of Action française, about the advent of the forty-hour workweek and paid vacations, or about the appeal of sleek sports cars and the new speed of airplanes—he looks to detail as he had along the Alladian Lagoon. Noteworthy are the remarks on the unconscious expression of individuals attending the departure of kin in the months preceding the declaration of war in September 1939. The way a woman clasps her hands behind her as she holds a purse, or the strange value that a bag tied by string *(un baluchon)* carried by a man hurrying to get out of frame (17, image on 630), indicate what *we cannot grasp* in the image. Or his study of the pensive distraction of a young woman on strike celebrating the victory of the Popular Front (16, image on 90) addresses an infinitesimal distance between what might be her thoughts and the moment of collective expression. "To us she seems personally present in the event, simultaneously a historical actor and a private soul whom we would like to get to know." Augé ends by remarking that our attraction to the pictures ought to be countered, first, by a resistance to a "distanced" and condescending view of the lives and times of the people; and second, by the knowledge that fatality of a "vengeful god" was inevitably hanging over their heads and assigned them to a tragic fate of which they were unaware. And too, the display of anti-Semitism and fascism, so far from us, it would appear in the black-and-white pictures, ought not to be thought of as history, for each and every person (and Augé is wont to study individuals in anonymous masses, and not the household names of authors, filmmakers, and comedians seen in many of the pictures) at the time, like ourselves, "wanted to believe in happiness and dared not imagine the future" (30).

It may be that the need to "believe in happiness" links the work as a whole to an art of living, so apparent and commanding in the writings following the studies of Alladian cultures, to what Augé had called *ideo-logic* in the late 1960s. If anthropology is a viable discipline that can help us to cope with forces beyond our control or to engage as best we may in local and partial ways, it ought to be oriented toward what we might, if a "total" social fact can subsist after the deconstruction (that Augé performs) of the ambition and the ruse of Mauss's concept, call a theory of happiness. If most individuals, defined, like the riders of subways, by the others whom they are, succeed in living in a world severely compressed and despatialized, their success would be on the grounds of what he sees in the lives of the nameless people chronicled in *Paris années trente*. It is seen in these Parisians' willingness to hold to frail moorings of happiness and affirm a sociality assuring viable cultural process.

It is not by chance that Augé's first major piece of creative writing, a work that departs from the format of disciplinary inquiry, is built over a theory of happiness. *La Traversée du Luxembourg*[19] seems to draw a line of divide between research led "there," in Africa, and "here," in Paris. After *Le Rivage alladian* and *Théorie des pouvoirs et idéologie,* the author continued along the lines of inquiry opened in the work on sorcery, in *Pouvoirs de vie, pouvoirs de mort* (1977), and in a first treatment of the virtues of anthropology construed as everyday practice in *Symbole, fonction, histoire: Les interrogations de l'anthropologie* (1979). He then published *Génie du paganisme* (1982), and signaled the advent of a literary calling in the title that plays against the Romantic writer-chronicler François-René Châteaubriand's *Génie du christianisme.* With *La Traversée du Luxembourg,* an "ethno-novel" recounting a day in his life, the writer blends fieldwork in and outside of France with autobiography "considered from the angle of customs of theory and of happiness." The self of the anthropologist is scrutinized by the self of the writer. In this work are sketched the first lines of the research taken up in *In the Metro.*

It may be fitting to reserve commentary on *La Traversée du Luxembourg* for the Afterword in this volume on Augé and the subway in general. If he draws himself into the field of his ethnological inquiry, it is no less fitting for his readers to broaden the scope of appreciation of the work for riders of other subways and other trains of thought, that is, for other selves who confront the solitude and isolation of existence in the subterranean communities of urban transit in other cities and other cultures.

In the Metro

Memories

The first German soldier I remember seeing was at Maubert-Mutualité in 1940, upon return from the exodus. Until then the Germans had only been an immaterial and diffuse presence imposing endless shifts and revisions on our itinerary. We fled ceaselessly, but they were always ahead of us. Except for an airplane—and I especially remember the mix of fear and curiosity that came with the din when it buzzed over the flatlands of Champagné not far from Le Mans—no sign was apparent of a progression that, nonetheless, everyone was talking about. It was a blurred absence, an abstraction forever on the point of materializing—which happened only on the morning of the return, at the Maubert exit, at the square that was being crossed (at least I have always sensed this impression intact in my memory) by the hurried silhouette of a man wearing a gray soldier's cap.

It is clearly a Parisian privilege to use the subway map as a reminder, a memory machine, or a pocket mirror on which sometimes are reflected—and lost in a flash—the skylarks of the past. Yet, assembled impressions of this kind (the luxury of an intellectual having more free time than others) are not always so deliberate. Sometimes the chance happening of an itinerary (of a name, of a sensation) is enough for distracted travelers suddenly to discover that their inner geology and subterranean geography of the capital city meet at certain points, where dazzling discoveries of coincidences promote recall of tiny and intimate tremors in the sedimentary layers of their memory. Certain subway stations are so associated with exact moments of my life, nonetheless, that thinking about or meeting the name prompts me to page through my memories as if they were a photo album: in a certain order, with more or less serenity, complacency, or boredom, sometimes even with heartfelt emotion—the secret of these variations belonging as much to the moment of consultation as to its object. Now it happens that I rarely go by Vaneau or Sèvres-Babylone without pausing to think about my grandparents who lived during the war at a point almost equidistant between the one stop and the other, in a building whose modesty, for me, later radiated with prestige after I learned that André Gide had been living on the same street, the rue Vaneau, long after they had left, and when their apartment for me was no more than a distant memory; its windows used to look out onto the courtyard and, beyond, onto the garden of the Hôtel Matignon, protected from the curious gaze of outsiders by an immense green metal fence with a tightly knit ironwork webbing that, however, did not distract me from uninterrupted observation of the spectacle of moving guards patrolling the walkways with their heavy steps. From Maubert to Vaneau the habitual comings and goings of my childhood mapped out my territory, and the chance of existence (or some secret personal gravity) had it that the Gare d'Orléans-Austerlitz-Auteuil line, now extended to Boulogne, would always play in my life, in some way, a crucial role.

For a long time, for me the unknown had begun at Duroc, the beginning of a series of names of which the last was the only one I could recall: Porte d'Auteuil, because we occasionally got off there on Sundays to walk to the park or on the grass of the racetrack. In the opposite direction, Cardinal Lemoine (who could that cardinal have been?) and Jussieu, whose location and outer appearance were familiar, given their proximity to our home, were, seen from below, only names without any real content, required points of passage along the way to the Gare d'Austerlitz where we had disembarked in 1940 and from where I was dreaming one day to leave. Later, on this line that I could indeed call a lifeline (but on a subway map I read only the past), other stations played an important role for reasons tied to age, work, and residence: Odéon, Mabillon, Ségur filled gaps, complicating but scarcely extending the territory of my childhood.

When I reflect on it a bit, this territory is not the simple sum of my wanderings and personal memories: a social pattern, rather, broadly determined in principle by my parents' desire, that indeed was drawn from another story, their own, I might say, since it is also somewhat my own and, besides, it largely escaped the decisions they forced themselves to take freely. As always, history came from elsewhere, punctuated with events that are said to be historical (because those who live them are sure about not being their masters) and yet whose savor appears irremediably unique to each and every one among us, despite the banality of the words that tell it, of the situations in which it is rooted, and of the dramas that make up its plot while endlessly threatening to undo it (that's life . . .). In a word, subway stops were everywhere in my educational, professional, and familial life; about this "civil status" I can recognize a few of these exact, somewhat disembodied words, like those used in a curriculum vitae. In that way my itineraries resemble those of others with whom I rub shoulders every day in the subway without knowing where they went to school, where they lived and worked, where they are at, and where they are going, while at that very instant our glances meet and turn away after sometimes lingering for just a moment. They too are possibly drafting an inventory or making a summary—who knows?—contemplating a change of life and, by extension, a change of subway lines.

For subway lines, like lifelines on the hand, meet and cross—not only on the map where the interlacing of their multicolor routes unwinds and is set in place, but in everyone's lives and minds. It happens, moreover, that they intersect without crisscrossing, as do the wrinkles of the palm: by making a point of being unaware of these superb and monochrome lines, linking once and for all one point to another without being distressed by the more discrete ramifications allowing whoever borrows them to change direction radically. In the vocabulary of the subway rider, to do this "you have to change twice." Thus it would suffice for the rider, leaving Ranelagh or Muette, who might be afraid to go to Strasbourg-Saint-Denis, to change successively at Trocadéro and Charles de Gaulle-Étoile to get back to better kempt neighborhoods where he or she started out, in the direction of the Porte Dauphine or, to the contrary, heeding the call of some mischievous or working-class rogue, to embark in the opposite direction toward Pigalle or Jaurès.

As for me, I am well aware that there might be some illusion to imagine my life as a rectilinear path because of my devotion to the Auteuil-Gare d'Orléans-Austerlitz line. For, if I never completely abandoned it, I did know, in the course of my Parisian years, other regular circuits, other routines, other litanies (Pasteur, Volontaires, Vaugirard, Chaussée d'Antin, Havre-Caumartin, Saint-Augustin, Miromesnil . . .) whose endless and daily recall, like a prayer or a string of rosary beads, would briefly exorcise the earlier automatisms. At a given moment, each of these itineraries defined the different aspects of my professional and family life on a daily basis and imposed its repetitions and rhythms. The regular traveler on a given line is easily recognized by the elegant and natural economy of his or her way of walking; like an old sailor who calmly descends toward his boat at dawn and appreciates in a glance the billowing waves at the exit of the port, measuring the force of the wind without appearing to touch it, with style, but in a less studied way than a taster sniffing a glass of wine, listening without seeming to heed the waves slapping against the jetty or the clamor of the seagulls gathered on the shore or already scattering over the sea in little avid flocks, the seasoned traveler, especially if he or she is in the prime of life and strongly resists the desire suddenly to burst into the stairs for sheer pleasure, can be recognized in the perfect mastery of his or her movements: in the corridor leading to the platform, the traveler walks swiftly but without rushing; without letting on, all senses are on alert. When, as if surging off the walls lined with enamel tiles, the noise of an oncoming train becomes audible, disrupting most of the occasional riders, this traveler knows whether or not to hurry, either by assessing the distance to the boarding area and deciding to take a chance or not, or by having identified the source of the crescendo of din and heard in this lure (peculiar to stations where several lines intersect and which for this reason French calls *correspondances,* while Italian, more evocative and more precise, speaks of *coincidences*) a call from beyond, the deceptive echo of another train, the temptation of error brings an invitation to loiter. Once on the platform, he or she knows when to stop walking and determine the site that, allowing easy access to the doorway of the train, corresponds, furthermore, exactly to the nearest point of "his or her own" exit on the destination platform. It is seen among old habitués who meticulously choose their point of departure, get set and on their marks, like high jumpers, in a way, before they thrust their bodies toward their destination. The most scrupulous push their zeal to the point of choosing the best spot in the car, from where they can exit most rapidly as soon as the train pulls to a stop. More tired or older, a few try to reconcile this tactical imperative with the need to rest, and seek to grab the last folding seat with a mixture of discretion and swiftness that also marks the veteran subway rider.

The extreme precision of these mechanical gestures easily

recalls artisans who shape the objects of their craft. Subway riders basically handle nothing more than time and space, and are skilled in using the one to measure the other. But they have nothing to do with a physicist or a Kantian philosopher. They know how to adapt themselves to the resistance of matter and to the throng of bodies, in a single gesture grasping the door latch with a flick of the wrist, as might a self-centered brat smoothly slipping the ticket of his subway pass, into the narrow slot of the turnstile, glancing off the walls and cutting the last corner, jumping down the last stairs two at a time, before leaping through the closing doors of the car, escaping a hard knock on the ribs from the jaws of the automatic door and applying an insistent pressure with the forearms on the inert mass of those who, having just entered, don't think anyone else could ever get in behind them.

Traces of this virtuosity tied to habit are already found outside of the station, in the use of neighboring space plotted by a few remarkable points: café, bakery, newspaper kiosk, crosswalk, traffic light. Clearly remarkable points, but by which ordinary practitioners of everyday life pass without paying much attention, even if they usually stop at these places to warm up, to get information, or, in the last two instances, to test—even if they are of a capricious or argumentative disposition—their reflexes and power of acceleration.

Most of the singular itineraries in the subway are daily and obligatory. We don't choose to retain them or not in our memory: they get impregnated within us, like the memory of military service. Here we happen to be only a step away from imagining that on occasion these trips refer not only to themselves, but also to a moment of life suddenly perceived (in all illusion, perhaps) in its totality, as if the individual who consults a subway map were sometimes rediscovering the point of view (somewhat analogous to what André Breton postulated about the origins of the Surrealist vision) that allows the meanderings of private life, the vagaries of a profession, the sorrows of the heart, the political conjuncture, the travails of time, and the pleasures of life to become palpable in all their transparency, strangely solitary at a distance.

Surely it is our own life that we confront in taking the subway, and in more than one way. Our trips today cross over those of yesterday, a slice of life of which the subway map, in the schedule we carry inside ourselves, reveals only a piece, the aspect simultaneously the most spatial and the most regular, but about which we know well that everything was or seemed to be in order, no hermetic barrier separating, perhaps to our greatest misfortune, the life of the individual from that of others, our private life from our public life; our story from that of others. For our story is itself plural: the itineraries of daily work are not the only ones we held in memory, and the name of this or that station that, for a long time, was for us merely one name among others, a common point in an invariable series, could suddenly acquire a meaning, a symbol of love or of misfortune. Near hospitals one always finds a florist, an undertaker, and a subway station. To every station are tied knots of memories that cannot be untangled, memories of these rare moments, Stendhal used to say, "for which life is worth living." Of each of them, resembling the others in that it differs from them, the only ones in charge for a while are one or two unique consciences whose secret passion, formerly or recently, had to take the subterranean passages of the underground rapid transit. The ways of the metro, like those of the Lord, are impenetrable: they are traveled endlessly, but all this agitation acquires meaning only at the end, in the provisionally disillusioned wisdom of a backward glance.

To speak of the metro first of all means to speak of reading and of cartography. I seem to recall that in the history atlases of my childhood, pupils were invited to measure the alternating periods of growth and decay in France: France before the Revolution, France under the First Empire, France in 1815, France under the Second Empire, France after 70 . . . There is something of an accordion effect in the image of my life presented to me by a subway map. But even more (here one needs to refer to other plates of the atlas: geological France, agricultural France, industrial France . . .), several maps of reading might be distinguished (amorous life, professional life, family life . . .), themselves, of course, related to a few crucial dates. All these distinctions would furthermore not prevent some recapitulation; it would probably be possible, just as one analyzes the different periods of a painter's life (blue or pink, figurative or abstract . . .), to demarcate in the lives of many Parisians successive "periods," such as a Montparnasse period, a Saint-Michel period, and a Bonne-Nouvelle period. Each of them (we know well) would surely correspond to a more secret geography: the subway map is also the Carte du Tendre or the open hand that one has to know how to fold and study closely in order to blaze a trail from the lifeline to the headline onto the heartline.

At this point a paradox emerges. Isn't the first virtue of personal recollections, inspired by a somewhat dreamy consultation of the subway map, that of having us sense something like a feeling of fraternity? If it is surely true that by daily trips in the Parisian rapid transit we constantly brush up against the history of others (during rush hour, parenthetically, this expression is obviously a euphemism) without ever meeting it, nonetheless we could never imagine it to be that different from our own. This paradox is solid enough to give pause to the ethnologist because it brings forward yet another; it even, perhaps, in my judgement, provides the same person with a means of resolving or illuminating it. The paradox familiar to the ethnologist is the following: all "cultures" are different, but none is radically foreign or incomprehensible to the others. At least that is how I would formulate the problem. Others would stick to the first part of the proposition and lay stress either on the absolutely irreducible and ineffable character of each singular culture (thereby adopting a relativistic point of view), or on the biased, approximate, and vulnerable character of all the descriptions, all the ethnographic translations (hence assigning to ethnological inquiry a long detour through the laborious but rock-solid methods of experimental disciplines such as cognitive psychology). In its period of conquest, ethnology held fewer scruples; in the name of culture it brought together very heterogeneous elements (tools and diverse objects, forms of matrimonial alliance, pantheons, and religious practice . . .) and unabashedly turned them into signs of evolution, even when it admitted the circulation of these "traits" from one society or culture to another. It invited the ethnologist to be as skeptical of ethnocentrism as of the absorption by the milieu. It enjoined the ethnologist at once to keep his or her distance and to engage in participatory observation, condemning the ethnologist to schizophrenia because it took for granted the gift of ubiquity.

The experience of the subway (and a few others, I must admit, but the subway is exemplary) inspires me to replace what might be called the paradox of the Other (spelled with an uppercase O because we are dealing with the cultural Other) with the paradox of two others (spelled with a lowercase o because, as soon as they are two, this duality of needs relativizes the absolute character of the former). At this point, I should like to open a new parenthesis and offer a personal example in order to clarify the issue. I have never understood what it meant to be a "believer." My mother is a believer, my aunts are believers, and a few cousins and uncles too. As for me, not at all. But let's be clear: I like them, I respect them, I respect their belief, I don't begrudge them celebrating their Easters or going to Mass, but I don't envy them either; my indifference is total, animal, and definitive. If in this regard I felt a lack, I could speak of frigidity, because, of course, Catholicism is my culture: I was made to do all that was required throughout my childhood, without the slightest abusive insistence, moreover, such that I can't even attribute my incomprehension to some effect of metaphysical excess, of clerical overdose, or of liturgical satiation. No, I have always been without imagination and clueless before the spectacle of those who seemed to take it for granted that I was a believer. The conversations I shared with my circle of friends at a time when, as an adolescent, I still had discussions of this kind, in some way deepened my incomprehension: that one had to believe in something I could admit, but why one dogma instead of another? And how! The most painful thing was, in fact, that I understood the process itself as little as I did its object. Especially incomprehensible for me were those who informed me that dogma had to be taken or left, that the main thing was personal, reasoned, intimate faith, whatever. And anyway, I was always rather sensitive to the splendors of the church, to the charm of the hymns and the memories of my summer vacations in Brittany. I could surely understand why people might go to church for the pleasure of it. But, in all probability, believers have something else in mind.

The incomprehension was, apparently, reciprocal. "What? You don't believe in anything?" a cousin asked me one day, but I didn't succeed in making her realize that those who added something (who not only "believed" but believed "in something") needed to make themselves clear, if they believed they were capable of doing so. I would not swear that I did not experience some malicious pleasure in playing the role of a libertine in front of my cousins, but I never had the feeling of either forcing or of artificially fortifying my mind: in my heart I was discovering, without excessive astonishment, that after all was said and done, my education had prepared me for . . . alterity.

The other begins close by oneself; it should even be added that in many cultures (all have constituted anthropologies, representations of man and of humanity) the other begins with the self, and without the benediction of Flaubert, Hugo, or Lacan. The plurality of elements that defines the self as a composite, provisional, and ephemeral reality—the product of diverse heredities and influences—therein appears so essential that the labors of ethnologists, whether relativistic or not, always dedicate to the very problematic notion of the individual an entirely indispensable chapter on the understanding of those who deal with economy and social organization.

But let's be done with the lineal subtleties and the complexities of the self and get back to the subway. Everyone I meet there is other, in the full sense of the term: it's worth wagering that a sizable number of my occasional companions have beliefs or opinions whose language I don't even understand (statistics and polls might allow me to back up this assertion with precise statistics), and I am obviously not speaking of foreigners and those whose skin color could lead me to believe that they belong to cultural milieus other than mine. I would even dare to suggest—but that is perhaps a too relativistic presumption on the part of the ethnologist—that I would more easily identify with the analyses, the fears, and the hopes of someone from the Ivory Coast (I know some who, like myself, get off at Sèvres-Babylone) than with the deepest thoughts of my next-door neighbor, with whom I sometimes ride for a while, and who reads *La Croix*.

What are the most frequent reproaches leveled at ethnologists? To heed the words of a small number of informants, to not beware of speech, and to generalize for a totality of societies what they are incapable of establishing with certitude for a single one among them. I will pass on what might be unfair and inexact in the detail—and thus in the sum—of each of these accusations, of which a certain degree of pertinence cannot really be contested, by simply remarking that in this respect every individual would be perfectly unknowable to the other and that, properly speaking, no acquaintance of people through people would be possible. And if perchance someone retorted to me that I am mixing genres, that I am applying to interindividual relations a critique that holds for intercultural relations, I would respond with two questions: Isn't cultural relativism based precisely on a critique of language and especially of the communication between informants and those informed, that is, between individuals? By suggesting that cultures cannot be partially or totally translated from one to the other is not cultural relativism reified—especially when it is admitted that within a given culture communication is transparent, words are unequivocal, and alterity is absent? In *Race and History*, Lévi-Strauss underlined that primitive peoples could not be considered as children (of a humanity itself conceived as evolutive), quite simply because they bore children and labored to shape them into adults.[1] Why not affirm the idea that in every society others exist (and there is much more at stake) and that this simple observation relativizes both the definition of the levels or the strictly "identitarian" thresholds (generations, classes, nations) and relativism itself? Others are not so irreducibly other that they do not possess an idea of alterity—a remote alterity, to be sure (of foreigners), but also of immediate alterity (of their immediate kin).

The signs of immediate alterity are frequently encountered in the subway, and are often provocative and even aggressive. And yet still I omit the instances of those that pertain to remote alterity and attest to the irruption of global history in our daily rides: Asians heading to the Place Maubert to stock up on goods or going over to the Place d'Italie, Africans from the Maghreb or sub-Saharan Africa going in the direction of Anvers or sweeping the corridors of Réaumur-Sébastopol, Americans or Germans noisily going off in groups to visit the Opéra. Immediate alterity (but alas, it is already somewhat remote!) is first of all that of young people or, as they say on television, "the young." Young people: those whose youth above all means in the eyes of others that their own has passed. Some wear a ring in their ear or dye a lock of their hair bright green. These people are both the most bothersome and the most familiar, resembling the image of them that we figure for ourselves—because it is ubiquitously reproduced in the newspapers and in advertisements— and that for the same reason they want to ascribe to themselves. We might find this process of identification disconcerting, but it cannot be surprising, for we have analogues of our own. As Johnny Hallyday, a star whose already long career requires—or will soon require—a makeover of his image (even and especially if he is wise enough not to change his "look," the day he has the curiosity to stare into the mirror he holds up to others he will discover people of his age) used to put it so well: "An idol is only a guy that kids want to look like."[2]

Because it draws us into quotidian humanity, the subway

plays the role of a magnifying mirror that invites us to take account of a phenomenon that, without it, we might risk or perhaps try to be unaware of: if the world, in its majority, is getting younger, we are the ones moving away from it. What are still for us current events have already become history for others. Surely it is painful to have believed oneself the idol of youth and to discover that one is the Tino Rossi of the almost-old or of the new-old guard. But that is a fundamental and exemplary experience: at the very moment when our own history catches up with us, that of others escapes us. I say "us" with a kind of sympathy for people of my generation, who must at one time or another perceive as I do the unusual optical effects created by placing into parallel alignment histories moving at different speeds: our personal history speeds up ("it's crazy how time flies . . .") while young people have time on their hands or even get impatient in their initial meanderings (and it is true that they have to finish their studies or find a job, find their bearings, decide on a career, get settled . . .); but from another point of view the inverse takes place: they leave us where we are, and in confusion we feel that it is they who are making or are going to make history. No doubt politics and the economy are always, and for a moment, in more respectable hands. But those hands, if I may say so, rarely meet in the subway, or they do so discreetly.

Clearly, the young are not youthful in the same way. Their respective destinies are not measured by the number of rings in their ears or dyed locks of hair on their heads. Something even upsetting occurs on Friday or Saturday evenings around République or Richelieu-Drouot when Indian youth of the popular classes take the path of their reserves, sporting all the conventional signs of stereotypical originality. What do they have in common with these girls springing directly out of the bourgeois haunts of my adolescence whom I meet now and again around Ségur or Saint-François-Xavier, who wear with a discretion—itself laden with meaning—blue blazers over their pleated plaid skirts?

What they have in common, and what evidently does not

impede them from being as different from one another as their origins and probably their respective destinies, is their relation to time, which radically distinguishes them, for example, from people of my age. The people of my age: we might be led to believe that they too constitute a false, and in some way negative, community, defined by default, by the number of years spent, washed away (as they say of color having faded), and, in the eyes of an ideology of modernity, passed by. We all have our points of reference, our own pasts that can be as different as our presents. Like these solitary sailors hidden from one another by the swell of the sea, but to whom the radio reports that they are staying on course, almost neck and neck, "in a photo finish," we feel ourselves in proximity only through the words of others. The past that we share is an abstraction, or better, a construction: it happens that a book, a magazine, or a television broadcast tells us what we were living at the time of the Liberation or during May 1968. But then who is this "we" to whom the meaning of what has passed should be directed? In a word, who is not Stendhal's Fabrice at Waterloo?

Surely Waterloo could only have its name given to a railway station or a subway stop in London. This observation itself bears a historical value, but even more so a cultural one. For does the presence of the name of "victories" in the subway (Austerlitz, still again, Solférino, Bir-Hakeim) signify the copresence of history in our everyday lives or the irreality of history? Is it this history that acquires meaning, like that of individuals, only retrospectively (yet the quarrels of historians are not the least strident), this history that has been made by those not always being conscious of having lived it and of which none of those who believe they have lived it retain the same memory?

Here perhaps it would be better not to force the point: a generation, we know by intuition and experience, is really nothing. People of the same age do not fail to have common memories, or at least memories in common that, if they are different, still distinguish more clearly those who refer to them from those who at best have only a bookish knowledge of them. My daughters and I probably have the same relation to Solférino, but not to Bir-Hakeim, even if I wasn't old during the war. Durkheim (who, having never given his name to a Paris street, has no chance, a fortiori, of ever figuring on the subway map) considered commemoration and celebration a source and a condition of the sacred. There cannot be a society, he thought, "that doesn't feel the need to uphold and to affirm over and again, at regular intervals, the collective feelings and ideas that constitute its unity and its personality."[3] Within this relation, civil ceremonies did not appear to him to differ in nature from strictly religious ceremonies. But for Durkheim, these ceremonies are always ceremonies of memory, festivals of collective memory. "The only hearth of warmth that can enliven us morally is that which forms the society of our kin," he continued, but the combustible element that fuels the fire at this hearth is the shared past upheld and reanimated while being commemorated. Durkheim certainly knows, in fact, that the past is more efficacious for having been lived, and that dead pasts (the past of those who are deceased) are less likely to kindle the social fire—the one by which individuals warm themselves—than the past of the living. At times societies need to make over the past the way individuals make over their health. When Durkheim says "society," I often understand "generation," and it is incontestably of the malaise of a generation that he speaks at the end of *Les Formes élémentaires de la vie religieuse*: "The great things of the past, those that our fathers were enthusiastic about, do not arouse the same ardor in us, either because they have entered into common use to the point of being unconscious for us, or because they no longer respond to our current aspirations."

We discern the double and contradictory hypothesis that might thus suggest the historical "charge" obvious from travels in the subway. So many stations, so many situations or personages recognized, retained, and magnified. The train threads its way through our history at an accelerated speed; relentless, it commutes without fail and in both directions, among great people, high places, and great moments, passing without delay from Gambetta to Louise Michel, from the Bastille to Étoile or from Stalingrad to Campo-Formio and back again. Taking the subway would thus mean, in a certain way, celebrating the cult of the ancestors. But obviously, this cult, if it exists, is unconscious; many station names say nothing to those who read or hear them, and those to whom they have something to say do not necessarily think of the thing when they pronounce the name. If there is a cult, one could say it is a dead cult: far from confronting society today with its past and the individuals that mold it to their own history, subway trips disperse to the four corners of Paris men and women who are in a hurry or tired, dreaming of empty cars and deserted platforms, occupied by the urgency of their everyday life and spotting on the map they are consulting or the stations that go by nothing more than the more or less rapid flow of their individual duration, estimated only in terms of being ahead of or behind schedule.

It cannot be said, therefore, that we discover underground the origins of a new social élan, of solidarity, or even complicity. The names of the stops evoke, neither strongly nor adequately enough, the history they celebrate such that, from the intersection of their so-called common referent and the diversity of individual trips, something necessarily is born resembling a collective emotion. I nonetheless happened to perceive once the fleeting outline of an emotion of this type when, getting off at Porte d'Auteuil with a friend who was a soccer fan, I fell into step with the hurried but orderly crowd pushing in the direction of the Parc. Long before Porte d'Auteuil it was already easy to identify those in the car who were going to the game—not only the young people, a bit hot under the collar who were hanging on to their still unfurled flags or were interrupting the clamor of immediately recognizable groups with trumpet blasts, but also all those who were traveling more discreetly, alone or in twos or threes, and whose complicitously friendly gaze, when it met our own, expressed the fellow traveler's pure sense of sharing, the happiness of the moment, and the imminence of a pleasure anchored in habit. For habit is essential to the alchemy of sports pleasure, and the eye that endlessly verifies through side-long glances at the map placed above the automatic doors a cav-alcade of names, familiar to everyone (as if Javel could ever fail to follow Charles Michels and the Église d'Auteuil to come be-fore Michel-Ange-Auteuil) betray less the neophyte's hesitation than the believer's restless obsession. The game everyone is waiting for recalls first of all those that preceded it, and that is true even for the semifinals, which, after a year of hope, propel into the subway crowds filling the air with the strains of singing. Rare then are those who have not already gotten on at the Parc on a similar occasion and who do not get from this subway ride the best of the emotion they came to find: the happiness of be-ginning over and again. An allusion to Porte d'Auteuil can be heard only by enlightened fans who, having already been to the Parc, know that one day or another, they'll meet once again in the train on the Porte d'Auteuil-Boulogne line.

If it is true that everyone has a past of his or her own, it none-theless happens that some, those who remember having lived fragments of their past with others, can sense they have shared at least this memory with them. They have in common—and they know it—this movement of the mind that, on a few very specific occasions, draws toward the past a glance directed to the pres-ent, conferring on the latter a kind of rare and heartfelt timeless-ness. The complicity that can emerge from this parallelism—no matter how capricious and subjective memory may be—some-times materializes unexpectedly, in a serendipitous meeting or along a detour in conversation ("Oh! really! Did you know him too? . . . Now let's see, that must have been in 19 . . . 66 or 7, no, 67, I think . . ."), but the subway routes provide the rider with stable points of reference and, when combined with the calendar of sporting events, regular time frames.

It also happens that an individual memory gets confused with more general commemorations, as a result emphasizing the symbolic value of the name that suddenly refers at once to the collective event and to an individual presence. For a number of reasons, Fabrice did not take the subway to Waterloo, but there probably exists more than one traveler likely to remember him and others when they go by Charonne. One would have to have lived like me, at the intersection of the boulevard Saint-Germain and the rue Monge, and be at least my age, to associate Maubert-Mutualité and Cardinal Lemoine with the battles of the Liberation and with the Leclerc Division, but other names, clearly enough, awaken in other individual consciousnesses memories that are not only personal. Certain names are dazzling enough to recall in themselves the military pageantry that occasionally bedecks them (Champs-Élysées-Clemenceau, Charles de Gaulle-Étoile), while others bring immediately into view the image of the monuments they designate or with which they are associated: Madeleine, Opéra, Concorde.

Yet still, historical consciousness prevails—one that forces upon us both the changes of names of stations and their fidelity to the past. Like streets, stations, as a function of current events, can change their names, the latter being generally only for the places they serve. To the glory of celebrity, the subway map brings, furthermore, subtle nuances and consecrates certain names only by mentioning the artery or the square to which they are attached, as if it found something repugnant about distinguishing them a second time, satisfaction being gained by confirming a required site of passage that does not engage its responsibility.

The further it moves away from the capital, the more the metro seems to lose a sense of history (the R.E.R. bringing this oblivion to its ultimate end) in order to take refuge in topography. Thus the names Malakoff-Rue Étienne-Dolet, and Carrefour Pleyel, or Boulevard Victor and Boulevard Masséna (on the R.E.R.) seem to hold at bay names they underline geographically more than historically. Furthermore, the network grows ceaselessly, extending its branching lines beyond metropolitan Paris stricto sensu, acquiring in the process names that in the eyes of the traditional Parisian are perfectly exotic (Les Juilliottes, Croix-de-Chavaux) and sometimes subtly romantic because they evoke at once ideas of frontiers and departures (Saint-

Denis-Porte de Paris, Aubervilliers-Pantin-Quatre-Chemins).
Franklin D. Roosevelt quite naturally found his niche on the
Champs-Élysées between Clemenceau and Étoile, but it is quite
remarkable that the graft of Charles de Gaulle onto Étoile took
so quickly and so well.

Double names are not rare in the metro, but their origins are
diverse; most often they designate an intersection (Réaumur-
Sébastopol) or two proximate spots (Châtelet-Les Halles). The
originality of Charles de Gaulle-Étoile (albeit relative, since
the same coupling had been at the origin of Champs-Élysées-
Clemenceau) is owing to the juxtaposition of the names of a
man and a place-name. The exceptional success of this composite name (it was quickly applied to designate the station itself or
the line for which it stands as the terminus and that departs
from Nation, whereas the Place de l'Étoile itself is rarely designated by its official full name) is probably the result of a series
of fortuitous meetings, including the one associating Nation
with de Gaulle, but also of the very particular use that is made
with metro words.

The silhouette of de Gaulle walking down the Champs-
Élysées from Étoile to Concorde, to the Liberation, a radiating
physiognomy, a haughty gaze joyfully shed upon the ground
has been sufficiently diffused and has symbolized rather spectacularly the mixed ideas of disembarkment, Liberation, and
salvation to catch—in the photographic sense of the term—
several generations, even those who, though not contemporary
with the event, only knew its image by virtue of the newsreels
that were, moreover, restoring its true, ostensibly historical nature as a founding and mythic event. In this sense, the expression "Charles de Gaulle-Étoile" is a model of symbolic over-
determination perfectly suited to spark the imagination of
everyone and the memory of many.

But it must be added that if it is used effectively, it is above
all because of the very particular respect we give to names sanc-
tified by the subway, even when we are unaware of their meaning. In keeping with names of individuals, we can note that,

consecrating a use about which we might be given to pause, the R.A.T.P. sometimes uses the name preceded by first name, and sometimes the last name alone. Thus we have a series of the order of Anatole France, Victor Hugo, Charles Michels, Félix Faure, and another of Garibaldi, Monge, Goncourt, Mirabeau, or Le Peletier; and if we happen to say "Sèvres" for Sèvres-Babylone (a familiarity that pays homage to the importance of the station, for it goes without saying that Sèvres alone could never designate Sèvres-Lecourbe, whereas Michel-Ange-Auteuil and Michel-Ange-Molitor are of equal dignity) or Denfert for Denfert-Rochereau, never would we allow ourselves to treat subway heroes as vulgar colleagues and merely call them by one name alone, unless it be by metropolitan etiquette, or, even less, a fortiori, by their first name: we would never stoop to say Roosevelt, Félix, or Victor. It remains that if the couplets Charles de Gaulle-Étoile and Champs-Élysées-Clemenceau go better with each other than Montparnasse-Bienvenüe (despite the legitimacy of the homage thus rendered to Fulgence Bien-venüe as a founding and civilizing hero), the reason must be sought in history, in a history that still has something to say to us and that is not related to popular lithographic broadsheets—*images d'Épinal*—brought to mind by Alésia, Convention, and Iéna, or else, in the register of great men, Saint-Paul, Étienne Marcel, or Cambronne.

As for historical fidelity, it is expressed in the name of certain stops that have refused to give way to current taste, such as Trocadéro, in complete disregard for the dated modernism of the Chaillot Palace, or Chambre des Députés, of which the sound of "Third Republic" fits with the decor kept up on the faubourg Saint-Germain.

Now if we often go without thinking from Bastille to Alésia, from Marx Dormoy to Pasteur, or from Saint-Augustin to Robespierre, if habit can even inure us to an image of Paris that certain names ought to suffice to evoke (Ménilmontant or Pigalle, Cité or Pont-Neuf, Mirabeau or Porte des Lilas) because they mix in the memories of Parisians that of refrains they have hummed, pages they have read, or films they have seen, it is nevertheless true that the slightest incident can bring back an awareness of our cultural or historical belonging. The authorities, as is their duty (at least in the conception made of them in France), dedicate themselves to bringing this memory to life by intelligently decorating the interior of stations such as Louvre, changing travelers into subterranean viewers of reproductions whose originals they should thus be more legitimately tempted to see above ground. But foreign tourists, especially those who circulate in groups and talk boisterously, are in this respect the most efficient. Hearing them appreciate the copies exhibited on the platform of the Louvre station or exclaim with delight "Opéra!" or "Bastille!" when the train stops beneath these exalted places carries some consequences not devoid of ambiguity. They embody our history; it exists because they greet it. At the same time, to some degree we play a role in the decor, like a Greek near the Parthenon or an Egyptian next to the Pyramids— all individuals for whom, when we are tourists, we would readily think the Parthenon or the Pyramids must be on the top of the list of their preoccupations since, in our eyes at least, these monuments define them in their ethnic or cultural singularity. Under the tunnel, we are the ones who were looking at the tourists with a slightly bemused indulgence; arriving at the station, and simply because its name, pronounced with the foreign accent of an outside observer, restores all of its historical aura, here we are assigned to a decor and a role, as routine witnesses, condemned to suggest, by a raising of our eyebrows or a vague smile, the past of the Bastille or the chic of the Opéra, to proclaim, because it is imposed upon us, the originality of our history and of our culture.

And if perchance one of these foreigners were inclined to ask us of the origin and meaning of some of the best-known names of the metro (Alma-Marceau, Denfert-Rochereau, La Motte-Picquet . . .), we would probably want to slip away, like these old villagers whom the ethnologist stubbornly tries to get to say why initiates to this or that god wear a red feather in their hair or why the god they serve is so named and not otherwise, and we would generally respond to our overzealous interlocutor, with no more duplicity or ill will than these old villagers, that we haven't the slightest inkling, that we've always known them without having a clue about them, even if it surely appears to us along the way that Marceau was a revolutionary general and that Alma has something to do with the story of a Zouave.

It is thus not absolutely true that metro travelers never have anything in common or that they have little occasion to perceive that they are sharing with others a few historical references or some shards from the past. But this experience is itself rarely collective. The metro is not a site of synchronism despite the regularity of many people's schedules: each person celebrates his or her holidays and birthdays; each biography is singular, and the moods of the same individual are variable enough that a collective effervescence will not bubble forth at the Concorde or Bastille stops outside of the moments when some special celebration (a meeting against racism, an election) happens to render to these place-names the prestige and force of emotion they hold with the past. In ordinary routine, shattered sacrality is what one should speak of (each person travels in search of his or her own history), or of ritual sacrality insofar as the rite survives what it commemorates, surviving memory to the point of no longer being suited to the slightest exegesis, an empty form that might be taken for dead if History (with a capital H: the history of others perceived for a moment as the history of everybody) did not, from time to time, renew its meaning. Thus we sometimes see in Africa or in America the Christian religion taking over archaic ritual forms and giving them a new substance, without it being easy for the observer to decide whether form or substance is winning out, and to characterize the new religion, which very obviously cannot be reduced to the sum of its elements—a phenomenon that corresponds, moreover, to the secret of all birth.

We can certainly imagine taking the subway for pleasure, in search of emotions that everyone is likely to feel in passing. For some years now, a current of air of unknown origin sweeps through the corridors of Ségur, awakening, I imagine, for more than a few a nostalgia for the sea or ocean fury. At Concorde, in the long tunnel that links the Balard-Créteil line to that of Vincennes-Neuilly, an entrenched accordion player squeezes out airs of the postwar years ("Cerisiers roses et pommiers blancs" [Red cherry and white apple trees], "Les cigognes sont de retour" [The storks are back], "Le petit vin blanc" [The little white wine]) that will always have a special savor for those who heard them at the time they were created. But one must above all admit that every day individuals borrow, so to speak, itineraries they have no choice but to follow, constrained by memories that are born of habit and that sometimes subvert it, brushing by, unaware of, but sometimes having an inkling of, the history of others, taking paths plotted with a collective memory turned trivial, whose efficacy is perceived only occasionally and at a distance. One day, on the shores of the Senegal River, in one of these villages whose metal roofs, more solid and durable than straw, are paid for by the salaries of immigrant workers in France, I was cordially met by a man who insisted on telling me that for several years he had lived near Barbès-Rochechouart. "Ah! Barbès-Rochechouart . . . ," I idiotically repeated. Then we began to laugh, both of us happy, it seemed to me, about this instant of friendship inspired by the mere virtue of a name.

Solitudes

Were we to speak of ritual in respect to subway trips, and in a meaning different from what the term takes in common expressions when it is devaluated, a simple synonym of habit, it would perhaps be on the basis of the following observation, which sums up the paradox and the interest of all ritual activity: recurrent, regular, and without surprise to all those who observe it or who more or less passively are associated with it, it is always unique and singular for each one of those who are more actively involved. The paradox and cruelty of the obituary pages, which we routinely pass over listlessly, happen when it baldly delivers to us the familiar name of a dead person we believed to be alive. It restores to us the presence of a face at the very moment when it skips over its reality, awakening our recognition only so that our object might slip away and deliver into the banal flow of things a sudden image shaded with a few personal memories.

The regularities of the metro are obvious and well established. Both the first and the last metro perhaps draw some poetic allure from being seen, thus assigned an immutable place in the order of everyday life, the two being symbols of the ineluctable character of limits, of the irreversibility of time, and of the succession of days. In terms of space, public transport is equally suited to a functional and more geometrical than geographical description. To go from one point to another, the most economical route is easily calculated, and one still finds in certain stations one of those automatic maps that offer the curious traveler, with the simple pressing of a button corresponding to the station he or she wants to get off at, a series of points of light where the user can read an outline of connected and contrasting lines (each subway line having its own color) showing the ideal itinerary. As a child, I was fascinated by these games of light and occasionally made the most of a few instants of freedom given to me by my mother's distraction when she used to converse with one of her lady friends in the calm of traffic between rush hours. Then I could invent circuits whose wealth I measured according to the abundance of the monochromatic series that the electric maps allowed me to link, the ones with the others, like so many garlands of lights on Bastille Day.

Children today have other games, otherwise more complicated than the elementary combination exercises in which I formerly indulged, more for the pleasure of my eyes than any taste for calculus, and the electric push-button maps probably no longer exert on today's youth the charm they owed more or less to a technological modernism that today is very dépassé. But the subway map is still indispensable for efficient underground travel, and the statements it authorizes are naturally expressed in impersonal terms that underline at once the general nature of the schema, the automaticity of its design, and the repetitive character of its use. In its written form, the infinitive with its imperative nuance confers on this impersonality the value of a rule: "To go to the Arc de Triomphe take the direction Porte d'Auteuil-Boulogne, change at La Motte-Picquet-Grenelle and get off at Charles de Gaulle-Étoile." It is the language of tourist guides of every genre, ranging from ecclesiastical ritual to directions for use, cookbooks, or treatises on magic. The oral prescription itself ("To go to Nation via Denfert you change at Pasteur") acquires the tone of impersonal generality; it is impossible to tell whether the familiar *(tu)* or the impersonal *(vous)* therein designates a singular subjectivity (our interlocutor of the moment, the one who is worrying about what direction to take) or a class of anonymous individuals (everyone who hypothetically might be conduced to follow this direction), as in expressions such as "You give them an inch" (a small space is opened between the thumb and index finger) ". . . and they'll take a mile!" (arms open wide) or "No matter what you do, they'll get you one way or another."

Against the backdrop of the metro our individual acrobatics thus seem to play a fortuitously calming effect in the destiny of everyone's daily lives, in the law of human actions summed up by a few commonplaces and symbolized by a strange public place—an interlacing of routes whose several explicit prohibitions ("no smoking" *[défense de fumer]*, "no entry" *[passage interdit]*) underscore its collective and ruled character.

It is thus quite obvious that if everyone has his or her "life to live" in the metro, that life cannot be lived in a total freedom, not simply because no freedom could ever be totally lived in society at large, but more precisely because the coded and ordered character of subway traffic imposes on each and every person codes of conduct that cannot be transgressed without running the risk of sanction, either by authorities, or by the more or less effective disavowal of other users. Democracy will incontestably have made great progress the day the most rushed or least attentive travelers, of their own accord, renounce using the entry corridor to exit, finally sensitive to the honor done to them by the appeal to a morality without constraint of the simple overhead placard stating "no entry" *[passage interdit]*. It must be admitted that certain people remain indifferent to it (most astonishing is that there are not more of them), and, with more or less alacrity or innocence, run the risk, after a scuffle of which they are the primary cause, of getting a vengeful thrust of the elbow from one of those who, myself included, still have a Rousseauian concept of freedom.

Transgressed or not, the law of the metro inscribes the individual itinerary into the comfort of collective morality, and in that way it is exemplary of what might be called the ritual paradox: it is always lived individually and subjectively; only individual itineraries give it a reality, and yet it is eminently social, the same for everyone, conferring on each person this minimum of collective identity through which a community is defined. It is such that the observer wishing to express most succinctly the essence of the social phenomenon constituted by the Parisian metro would have to take into account not only its instituted and collective character, but also for what it is in this character that lends itself to the singular elaborations and intimate imagination without which it would no longer have any meaning. In sum, the observer would have to analyze this phenomenon as a total social fact with the meaning that Mauss gives to this term and that Lévi-Strauss refines and complicates at the same time by recalling its subjective dimensions. He or she would be led to an analysis of this type as much by the massive, public, and almost obligatory character of subway use in Paris (which distinguishes it from some of its homologues throughout the world) as by the daily evidence of its simultaneously solitary and collective character. For such is, really, for those who take it every day, the prosaic definition of the metro: collectivity without festival and solitude without isolation.

Solitude: this would probably be the keyword of the description an impartial observer might be tempted to make of the social phenomenon of the metro. The somewhat provocative paradox of this assertion would simply be related to the need prompting this observer to write the word *solitudes* in the plural, signifying by the final "s" the *boundaried* character of the community imposed by the dimension of the subway cars (the container) and the work schedules that determine their being filled and emptied (the contained): a little too many people, and shoving—which can occasionally degenerate into panic—imposes contact, inspires protest or laughter, in a word, creates a type of relationship that is clearly aleatory and fleeting, but that embodies a shared condition; a little too few people, in the lazy warmth of a summer afternoon or the draining cold of a winter night, and suddenly, depending on age, gender, and mood at the moment, the solitary traveler can feel the exaltation stemming from the fact of apprehending for an instant, in all of its purity, the greatness of one's social condition (the authorities are at one's service, words regain a function and meaning) or, to the contrary, the anguish of seeing emerge from the other end of the deserted corridor, under whose vault strangely resound his footsteps, the Enemy, the Foreigner, the Petty Thief, the Rapist, the Murderer.

Solitudes change with the hours. The most emotionally moving metro, and maybe the most peaceful one too, is in the early morning, the first metro, the one that one day, on the Vincennes-Neuilly line, travelers take from the first high-speed or "TGV" train that arrives at the Gare de Lyon, but that more regularly is taken by different workers, recognizable by the kind of nonchalance created from boredom and habit with which they page through the newspaper or let their bodies slip onto the folding seats at the end of the car. Their bodies are best molded to the nonetheless uncomfortable shapes as if for a last break before stampeding to the ticket window or the workplace. In their metallic frame, this morning just like yesterday and a little while ago, a dog and a cat with a forlorn look invite the traveler (maybe the very one that dozes under their paws) not to forget to give them a delousing treatment.

I recall my very first metro. An unproblematic young man (by that I mean I posed no problem for others, especially my parents), at about age seventeen I had attended my first surprise

party just as I had, a few years earlier, attended my first commu-
nion: without passion, but with application not bereft of curiosity. This "party" really offered little surprise. It was, rather, a
kind of sports event whose character of a rite of initiation became especially apparent around four in the morning, when
there was nothing left to do other than wait until five-thirty,
while the girls were sleeping and the stench of English cigarette
smoke was weighing heavily in my slightly pasty mouth, and, behind the window on which I was leaning my forehead the winter night was still dark.

Later, the office hours evoke less than the first subway the
daily grind that Baudelaire depicts in "Le crépuscule du matin"
[Morning twilight] at the end of the *Tableaux parisiens*:

> L'aurore grelottante en robe rose et verte
> S'avançait lentement sur la Seine déserte,
> Et le sombre Paris, en se frottant les yeux,
> Empoignait ses outils, vieillard laborieux.

> [Aurora shivering in her dress green and rose
> Toward the deserted Seine then slowly arose,
> And somber Paris, rubbing her eyes,
> Grabbed her tools, as an old worker would arise.]

These lines do not awaken in me any single image, strictly
speaking, but rather a series of somewhat faded and dispersed
images that they at once have the power to bring together and
clarify: a period when the rue des Bernardins, like all the other
streets that cut into the ancient and compact mass of buildings
along the Seine—the rue Maître-Albert, the rue de Bièvre—
sheltered a number of artisanal shops that have now all more or
less become extinct: coal merchants, tapestry weavers, window
makers, chair stuffers, cutlery sharpeners, hosiery menders,
milliners, and ladies' tailors—a providence for women of the
petite bourgeoisie. Sometimes we passed through the street, a
bit furtively, bidding adieu to the more fitting sidewalks of the

boulevard Saint-Germain and the rue Lagrange in order to cross the Seine at the Tournelle bridge and to walk as far as the Hôtel de Ville, thus sparing ourselves the inconvenience of two changes, on Thursday, when we used to go to the Tuileries. Sometimes too (and these are memories that I more immediately associate with the idea of Sunday) we used to stroll along the quays, and from the height of the Tournelle bridge we would cast a glance on the (Sunday) painters who, having erected their easels much earlier and gifted with a certain imagination, would, in the middle of the afternoon, impose upon the spectacle of Notre-Dame seen from the square—reproduced thousands of times —the contrasted colors of a dawn or a dusk in pastel tones in which always dominated, it seems to me, Baudelaire's pinks and greens.

Because of the profound transformation at the end of which there are still workers in Paris, but fewer and fewer who live there, the metros at dawn fill up more spectacularly around the railway stations, especially Saint-Lazare, with a crowd that is in a hurry and concentrated ("concentrated" in at least two senses, for in this "concentrate" of a solitary crowd every individual seems driven and guided by the fixed notion of a schedule calculated down to the last second, and "concentrating," as might an Olympic sprinter, on attaining an objective). The same crowd arrives in the evening, but in the other direction, pouring out of the metro into the railroad station and from the city to the frightfully but correctly named "periurban zones," even if the extension of the R.E.R. tends to mask the reality of this segregation by locating the triage stations in the heart of the metropolitan machine. Around eight-thirty or a quarter to nine, the crowd is still dense but sociability is more evident: colleagues meet, hail each other, converse, and joke. The solitudes are not so sleepy. The voyeur, the ethnologist, then has at his or her disposal more assured points of reference. Ethnologists can make an inventory of newspapers, little individual flags unfurled without too much ostentation (*Libération, Le Figaro*—in the metro *Libé* wins over the latter, it seems—but also *Le Parisien libéré* and a few copies of *Le Monde* from the evening before) that allow them, if they direct their attention to the page the paper is opened to, to speculate about each reader's preoccupations, depending on whether they see the person absorbed by news items, sports, or the political fortunes of which they themselves retain some echo from listening to the morning radio or reading the same newspaper.

If we look more closely, we cannot fail to notice that the activities of the subway traveler are numerous and varied. Reading is still prominent among them, mostly (although some lines are more intellectual than others) in the form of comic strips or sentimental novels of the Harlequin genre. Thus adventure, eroticism, or rose water is poured into the solitary hearts of individuals who apply themselves, with a pathetic constancy, to sealing themselves off from those around them without missing their stop. Where will the thoughts of these readers' heroes wander as, without surprise, each link in the chain of successive stations passes by, thoughts made even more protean than by surrendering to the seductions of an image or a story? The question can be reversed according to a formula by a writer (Georges Perec) who ponders the fate of the text: "What becomes of the text? What happens to it? How is the novel perceived when it extends between two stops, Montgallet and Jacques Bonsergent? How is it that the text is chopped up the way it is, this concatenation interrupted by the body, by others, by time, by the daily rumble of collective life?"[1]

Others knit, do crossword puzzles or correct their papers. At first glance, it is easier to imagine who these people are because they are very obviously reducible to their activity of the moment, but they remain all the more remote behind this immediately identifiable facade in that they do not betray the slightest indication—whether indirect or partial—of their deliriums, their desires, or their illusions, absorbed as they appear to be by the need to solve the technical problems they are tackling. Still others, the youngest, are absorbed in listening to mysterious forms of music imperceptible to us except for a few squeaks caused by poor tuning. For the moment there is nothing more to imagine, even if the glazed look or the poorly contained frenzy of a body jerking now and then to rhythms that can only be called "inner" suggests to the astonished gaze of the passenger— who suddenly discovers himself or herself mute and clueless ("out of it," as they say today, and it really is a misunderstanding that is at stake here) something (but what?) of intimate emotions, of something vague in the soul, and of the madness of people listening to Walkmans.

There are also (a silent majority, in fact) those who do nothing, who merely wait, with apparently imperturbable faces on which the attentive observer (the distracted walker, the innocent voyeur) can nonetheless sometimes overtake the passing of an emotion, an uneasiness, or a memory whose reason or object will never be grasped. There is a narrow border here between the romantic imagination that enjoys interpreting, for example, the fleeting smile that a woman's face seemed to direct toward some inner interlocutor and the malaise everyone feels at the spectacle of an agitated person (in the metro these cases aren't rare) whose fractured words, sighs, and laughter are heard or whose pointless fury is sign enough that he can no longer compose or control his attitude. Here solitude is definitely held captive: the more the person seems to wish to have passengers bear witness to his distress, the more his neighbors avoid his gaze by looking furtively at one another with glances that are at once embarrassed and complicitous.

Can ethnology thus help us understand what is too familiar to us to not remain strange and, in the present case, shed light on the paradox that sums up our vague and immediate intuition: that nothing is so individual, so irremediably subjective, as a single trip in the subway (even if it is only a matter of a trip by an adolescent with an anodyne look, an anonymous silhouette whose tastes and colors, tics and style, haircut, and music we feel we recognize), and yet nothing is so social as one such trip, not only because it unfolds in an overcoded space-time, but also and especially because the subjectivity being expressed during the passage and that defines it on each occasion (each person has a point of departure, changes of line, and a destination) is an integral part, as are all the others, of its definition as a total social fact?

It can, it seems to me, providing it does not turn immediate alterity into a destiny apart, and insofar as its reflection on the *total social fact* primarily bears upon the relation between sociology and psychology. I therefore propose an excursion to my readers: a short detour through a few pages of *The Gift,* and then a change that will lead them to get off the Maussian line in order to change over a bit to that of Lévi-Strauss (they intersect), before returning with me to a daily study of the subway, in the station of the reader's choice.

Mauss spoke of total social facts (an expression that he preferred to that of general social facts) in respect to phenomena such as the potlatch or visits from tribe to tribe that involve the totality of society and its institutions. He has no trouble, in the case of Melanesian or American facts, showing how they are at once religious, economic, aesthetic, and morphological, morphology understood here in the strictly Durkheimian sense as referring to the permanent and official character of territorial or maritime paths that make them possible, and to the system of alliances that guarantees peace and security for its members. But the idea of totality is more complex than one might think; it is the linchpin of an affirmation reiterated by French sociology throughout the twentieth century: the more it is global, the greater its concrete character. If the general functioning is thus identified with the concrete, it is because an institution is never more concretely discernible than when it is operative; because, from this moment on, it can no longer be observed in isolation—at once because people are needed to make it function and because its functioning presupposes and puts into motion that of other institutions. Mauss can thus affirm what might rightly seem paradoxical: the concrete is what is complete (sociologists, he says, contrary to historians, are overcommitted to division and abstraction; now a revolution is needed, everything "must be reconstituted"), and this effort at reconstitution will authorize the comparison, or rather, the clarification, of universals: "these facts of widespread occurrence are more likely to be universal than local institutions or themes of these institutions, which are invariably tinged with local color."[2] The advantage of generality and the advantage of reality, as he calls them, are mutually reinforced.

A paradox, in fact, for the two defining terms (generality and reality) can only coexist if they are in a relative relation to each other. Whence the idea of "average" whose conception allows generalization, but about which it can be wondered if it concretely expresses the real. "We should follow [historians'] precepts and observe what is given. The tangible fact is Rome or Athens or the average Frenchman or the Melanesian of some island, and not prayer or law as such."[3] Damn! And damn again! We easily foresee the double difficulty paraded before us: will it be so easy, once these historico-sociological entities are reconstituted, to free them from their cultural reserve? And then, supposing they retain something concrete (who is the "average" user of the Paris metro, if not the abstract user to whom the administrative injunctions are addressed?), will this something necessarily borrow its color from a place and a period of time? Is it the Parisianism of my user that will provide, if I may say, the measure of his or her average character?

Meanwhile, we can now exit the metro for a moment and get to the comments that Lévi-Strauss makes about Mauss's deceptively limpid analyses. Lévi-Strauss trips over his feet, if the expression can be permitted, in his "Introduction to the Work of Marcel Mauss," and it is conceivable—even if it is not caused by this sole aspect of his reflections—that it inspires the somewhat stilted irritation expressed about them in Georges Gurvitch's cautionary "preface" (the French heading, *avertissement,* is well chosen) placed before Lévi-Strauss's introduction. Here I quote the last sentence with pleasure because it attests to a somewhat irksome lucidity, as they used to say during my childhood ("Your uncle is a little irked," a way of saying that his state of mind at the moment was, in this circumstance, in harmony with his deep nature), in view of the false innocence of a sacrilegious commentary: "The reader will find in Claude Lévi-Strauss's introduction an impressive image of the inexhaustible wealth of the intellectual heritage bequeathed by this great scholar, as well as a very personal interpretation of Mauss's work."[4] In 1950, they knew how to wrap praise in barbed wire.

Now, what exactly is so sacrilegious about Lévi-Strauss's commentary? Surely nothing emanating from a great respect for the author and the work. But the worst commentators (in other words, the most embarrassing) can be precisely those who read texts literally. Mauss posited the equation concrete = complete. With this reciprocal complete-concrete he incontestably makes apprehension work, as does Durkheim, by taking account of the feelings developed by people in groups: "We have been able," he writes, "to see their essence, their operation and their living aspect, and to catch the fleeting moment when the society and its members take emotional stock of themselves and their situation as regards others."[5] The beauty of this expression (who would not be moved by the way this allusion to the instant in which people "take emotional stock of themselves" strikes the right chord—even if we would be hard put to say what it strikes?) obfuscates the arbitrary nature of an equation that in itself has not been demonstrated and that might be somewhat clumsily summed up as follows: if social facts can be considered as things, it is because society can be considered as a totality of people. Mauss simultaneously proceeds to reify and to subjectivize society or the group, which explains that they can gain a self-consciousness (clearly, a collective consciousness) by distinguishing themselves from others, from other societies or other groups. We can nonetheless note that, even at the cost of a syntactic or a logical incoherence, his phrase ("the society and its members take emotional stock of themselves and their situation as regards others") would have been much more compelling if "others" had referred to the proximate other, to others who are part of the totality of people gaining a consciousness of themselves. It would suffice to squinch between "gain" and "consciousness" something like "each for oneself," in sum, to reintroduce into the analysis the *individual* subjective dimension so that it signifies that people only gain self-consciousness (individual consciousness of themselves as individuals) at the moment when they become conscious of their situation in respect to others, in other words, of their social situation—in short, that they only gain self-consciousness by gaining consciousness of others, that the only individual consciousness is social consciousness. If need be, this can be stated inversely, since a nonindividualized social consciousness would be only an abstraction or a myth.

Now, Mauss did not really say that, but in rereading him one has the feeling that he almost said as much, even if the terms *crowd, society,* and *subgroups* are always accompanied in his writing by the notions of "feelings," "ideas," and "volitions." The others in respect to whom people situate themselves at different levels of organization are in fact themselves clearly relative: the other of another subgroup is no longer an other if it is the group that is being assembled. In other words, even in the most objective and most highly institutionalized meaning of alterity, the same individual can be alternatively considered or not considered as an other; something of the other exists in the self, and what belongs to the self that is in the other is indispensable for the definition of the social self, the only one that can be formulated and fathomed.

Where Mauss writes "people" *[les hommes]*, as if the generality of the plural attenuated the concrete character of the word, Lévi-Strauss makes its appear that he had written "the individual"; for it is only with the individual, he tells us, that the three dimensions of the total social fact can be brought together: its sociological dimension, with its synchronic aspects; its historical or diachronic dimension; and its physio-psychological dimension. Lévi-Strauss is not thinking simply of the effects that certain events might have on physiology or the psychic apparatus of those who live them. Prompted, rather, by something that has also tortured novelists, he ties the particular character of the social sciences to the obligation in which they find themselves to define their object both as object and as subject, as a "thing" and as a "representation" in the language of Durkheim and Mauss. In other words, the subjectivity of those the ethnologists observe is part of their object. Lévi-Strauss has stated the point better than anyone, so his words are worth quoting: "An appropriate understanding of a social fact requires that it be grasped *totally*, that is, from the outside, like a thing but like a thing which comprises within itself the subjective understanding (both conscious and unconscious) that we would have of it, of being inexorably human, if we were living the fact as indigenous people instead of observing it as an ethnographer."[6] The displacement that he has made is clear: part of the total social fact is the singular interpretation that each of its actors can give to it, or, more broadly speaking, each among those who are actively involved in it, and the resulting problem is simultaneously a problem of definition and of method. The problem of method is linked to what Lévi-Strauss calls the unlimited process of the subject's objectivation. By that we can infer that the ethnographer, condemned to account, in terms of external apprehension, for what he or she can imagine or relive of the internal apprehension of facts, of native experience, has to proceed by successive objectivations of his or her self, the task being facilitated by the fact that his or her object (societies and human groups) is at once familiar and remote. The thousands of societies that have existed or exist are human "and, for that reason, we participate in them in a subjective way." But, for another reason, all social experience is for us an object: "Any society different from our own has the status of object; any group of our own society, other than the group we come from ourselves, is object; and even every custom of our own to which we do not adhere."[7] The alternating or simultaneous efforts of identification, of projection outside of subjectivity and of reintegration into subjectivity, adds Lévi-Strauss, would run the risk of ending up with a misunderstanding (the ethnographer's subjective apprehension sharing nothing in common with that of the native), if the existence of an unconscious, with rules of its own, did not allow the opposition between the self and others to be overcome. The unconscious, "a mediating term between me and others . . . makes forms of activity that belong at once to us and to others coincide."[8]

But we know where Lévi-Strauss is going to look for signs of the unconscious: in the direction of systems and of their organization, whether social or linguistic. And the question can be posed as to knowing if, by finding the unconscious, he has not lost the individual, meaning the individual-individual, one of those who, living the total social fact, are each for their own part indispensable to its definition—about which it can readily be admitted, as a consequence, that it is strictly asymptotic, the sum of the actors being as little likely to be effected as the subjective apprehension of each one of them is interminable. It seems to me, moreover, that, in order to limit his critique of Mauss or to dissipate the vertigo liable to proceed from the theory of the unlimited process of the subject's objectivation, in 1950 Lévi-Strauss had placed culturalistic limits on his enterprise of destabilization. No sooner, in fact, had he written that the sole guarantee that a total fact might correspond to reality was that it could be grasped in a concrete experience than he illustrated the latter by examples drawn from Mauss; concrete experience was that "first of all of a society localized in space and time, 'Rome, Athens,' but also of any individual whatsoever in any one of these societies, 'the indigenous Melanesians themselves.'"[9] Now the Melanesian of some island has never defined "any individual whatsoever," an individuality, unless it is an individuality of a type or a culture; it should have been written, "a given Melanesian or no matter what Melanesian of some island." But Mauss (I quoted his exact formulation a bit earlier) did not write that; he was speaking of the average Melanesian, as of the French person of the same caliber, of culture and not of the individual, in such a way that Lévi-Strauss somewhat forces his hand (and somewhat forces the text), with some timorousness, nonetheless, either out of scruples for the text he is referring to, but that cannot, objectively, allow the commentary he is making about it ("the" Melanesian is not "a" Melanesian), or because, being less interested than he seems to suggest in the problem of the relation between the individual and society, between the self and others, he is already much more fascinated by the linguistic model that apprehends this relation on the basis of its instituted forms: language, rules, or myths.

How can the Parisian of this or that station be defined? And how can he or she be found? How can we admit that this person might be the key to what is concrete and complete? I see them go by every evening, at Sèvres-Babylone, squeezed like sardines in the subway cars or sprinting down the corridors—men and women, old and young, schoolchildren, secretaries, professors, employees, bums, Europeans, Africans, Gypsies, Iranians, Asians, Americans—all these subterranean travelers so different from one another, whose almost regular movements (like those of the Atlantic Ocean, with its high and low tides and its periods of strong or dead waters) suggest nonetheless that they are animated, shaken, tossed together, and dispersed by the same force of attraction. Is the only thing these multiple solitudes have in common—faces set by a tenacious preoccupation, febrile silhouettes, states of fatigue without appeal or boredom without disquiet, mixes of happiness and sadness whose unimaginably infinite multiplicity felt by turns according to the mood of the moment (the subterranean world, in sum, being able to pass for the metaphor of our inner worlds), like the expression of an immense indifference or the occasion of a secret affection—the not entirely fortuitous coincidence of their daily schedules?

To the contrary, we could think that through its resistance to any attempt to formulate a comprehensive definition, through an essential incompletion in the direction of things infinitely large and infinitely small, the social phenomenon of the metro—that underscores the limits of Mauss's analysis (beyond which it is revealed as contradictory or confused—can pass for a remarkable example of the total social fact. The very necessity in which we find ourselves speaking of "exploded sacrality" in respect to it would exemplarily underscore the impossibility of assimilating any kind of social phenomenon to the action and to the typical figure of an average subject. But the notion of total social fact cannot be reduced to the culturalist temptation that a somewhat distracted Lévi-Straussian gaze discerns in it, and the "abyssal" perspective that he discovers through the method of the "unlimited process of the subject's objectivation"—whether faithful or not is another story, in Mauss's thinking—offers a take that is inconvenient, surely, but unique and possibly decisive, for sociological analysis.

Mauss himself had admitted that a total social fact might apply only to a large number of institutions, not the totality of them, and individuals more than a collectivity: some of the total social facts "concern the whole of the society and its institutions (as with potlatch, opposing clans, tribes on visit, etc.); others, in which exchanges and contracts are the concern of individuals, embrace a large number of institutions."[10] In sum, but also in its Maussian sense, the total social fact possesses at least two pertinent traits. The first trait of a total social fact is that it is *at once* economic, juridical, and so on—in other words, it is irreducible to the language of an institution. Its second trait touches on its contractual or conventional character, which itself presupposes an explicit formulation and a consciousness that is at least implicit and not totally unconscious of the relation to others.

Now, travel in the metro, if defined in general as individual, is simultaneously and consistently contractual. The ticket can vary, and therefore the nature of the contract, between relatively restrictive forms, such as the weekly pass that assigns to its user a specific set of routes, and forms that are much more flexible and liberal, such as the monthly orange card, or the yearly card, that multiply the privilege (recognized for any ordinary ticket), authorizing its holder to travel underground as long as he or she wishes from the first metro of the day to the last. To my knowledge, this privilege is exclusively Parisian, and it can pass for an especially remarkable expression of the paradox that we encountered earlier: it is an individual freedom (even if it is limited by many other factors) that is purchased for the price of the ticket, which of course must be set according to imperatives of profitability that it is not entirely in good form today to say that they themselves ought to be limited by the imperatives of public service. The fact remains that this debate defines well, in political and economic terms, an institution of the metro whose most concrete expression is the actual possibility of a single free trip. Recourse to the orange card eliminates the sole constraint (but of stature) that weighed upon the traveler: the obligation of, if not interrupting a trip (because for the same price the person could always window-shop at the Louvre and ride the automatic walkway at Montparnasse-Bienvenüe), at least not leaving the space in which the freedom to circulate was allowed. "Beyond this limit your ticket is no longer valid" [Au-delà de cette limite, votre billet n'est plus valable], announced the panels at a time when the orange card did not yet exist, now replaced by a drier notice ("Limit of the validity of tickets" [Limite de la validité des billets]) that easily awards holders of the orange card the feeling of a lawful transgression.

In short, it is natural that the space of public transport is, as its name indicates, a contractual space in which is daily practiced the cohabitation of diverse opinions that, if they are not authorized to be shown off, are not obliged to be concealed, since some people in it read so-called newspapers of opinion, whereas others, who are surely not for all that forbidden to read the newspaper, display their hairdos, their badges, their medals, their uniforms, or their cassocks without, on the whole, on any daily basis, resulting in many confrontations. The theme of insecurity in the metro would not be so widespread, nor the reactions to any provocation or aggressive behavior so spirited, were not the idea of contractual consensus essential to the definition of this institution.

Economical, the space of the metropolitan rapid transit is (and spontaneously recognized as such by its users), to the point of inspiring a certain number of behaviors, complementary, or deviant and offbeat, that can be read or stated in the language of economy, even if they also have juridical, aesthetic, and social aspects. Two extremes: theft and cheating. Petty theft does not call for specific commentary: a minor variant of larceny, perhaps it draws its generally undramatic character from the conventional character of the place where it happens. Not that it has the same status as shoplifting at the Prisunic and department stores, in which some children of the young bourgeois of 1968 were able to practice for a time with a rather splendid innocence. The metro is still a traditional place; the modern petty thief, whether actually broke or not, is a reincarnation of yesterday's pickpocket; a minor figure, this person is not, in any case, whatever his or her age, an amateur. Theft is practiced at the margins of the system, and in that way differs from cheating. Given the current state of control mechanisms, cheating presupposes youth (it is hard to imagine an elderly man or woman flying over the turnstiles in a graceful leap) and, to state it in neutral terms, a certain state of indifference to the contractual character of subterranean transportation. An abstraction crafted from strictly financial causes or circumstances that can explain one particular way of cheating or another, the overall explanation of this behavior can probably be found either in an absence of good citizenship with many causes and expressions (but the absence of good citizenship is itself a sign more than a cause), or—and in this case the explanation would be more disturbing—in a certain bodily arrogance, the ability to jump over the turnstile being lived as its own legitimation, as if taking for granted the right to scorn the social contract; but it is not excluded that, in many cases, this mediocre performance participates in the illusion the weak have of not needing others because, in fact, they are entirely dependent on them. There again, the practice of the metro would be the expression of a certain state of society seen in one of its singular dimensions.

With cheating the pact is broken or refused, but whether it is a product of scorn, defiance, or deception, it acquires meaning only in relation to the pact. A site of heightened economic sensitivity, the metro permits observation of at least three other kinds of behavior that are clearly distinguished from theft and cheating. The latter are incontestably situated within the limits of a pact they are unaware of or that they contest; the former add to it, I daresay, and go beyond the pact, attempting to force passengers or passersby into a dual relation and a supplementary payment. Passing the hat is a way of imposing generosity: taking advantage of the enclosed space of the subway car, the singer or musician has about three minutes to perform and seduce. Perec had noted that the average interval of time between two stations was about a minute and a half and that reading in the metro could be organized according to this rhythm. This is even more true for the songs or guitar pieces that the performers have every interest in completing between a maximum of three stations if they don't want to lose their audience; thus they have an average of three minutes to use their talent to impose the idea of a necessary return gift, even if they are working in pairs, the second taking up the collection while the first is still singing or strumming. And it is true that talent often makes the difference: it is harder for passengers to avoid the feeling of reciprocity when they have been impressed by the beauty of a voice or the skill of an instrumentalist. A few signs very officially invite the public not to encourage this kind of spectacle, but in vain: today nobody is surprised by this anymore, even if the intrusion of two young people with a guitar in the subway car, in which everyone is thinking about the evening before and the next day, has the effect of enclosing a few solitary types a little more visibly in their determined avoidance of the world around them, either because they don't like music, or because they have no spare change, or because it is only in the metro that they appreciate an animal and relaxing feeling of intimacy with themselves, which they don't have the leisure to relish elsewhere and which all external contact arbitrarily dissipates.

Providing artistic services is different from passing the hat: occurring at a fixed spot, it is aimed at passersby, not at passengers; it imposes no dual relation, and does not underscore the necessary link between the gift and return gift. Judging by the quality of certain instrumentalists in the subway corridors, especially the classical ones, one realizes that many young professionals come there to practice—which would probably be more difficult for them to do at home, where, moreover, they would not pick up any money. And they do earn money. The way things are, those who least look like they're asking receive more—a deserving reward for an undeniable talent that a few people recognize and that many suspect, a gratuitous gift as well, given out of happiness and on the spur of the moment (African drums at Montparnasse, jazz at Odéon, Andean flutes or Bach at Sèvres—all help start the day off or get it going again), a gift close to alms as Mauss analyzes it—a gift to God more than solidarity among people?

A few beggars (as they used to say, for this term is disappearing) seem to have understood something about this and no longer beg, strictly speaking, but replace the singsong oral demand with a piece of cardboard or chalkboard that gives some information about their lot and their situation, resulting in a kind of begging "in silence," as they used to say about the first exchange among "primitive" peoples, but now relayed in writing. "I'm just out of prison, I need work." Unquestionably, whether they are true or false, these snippets of information are aimed above all at seducing the readers of *Libération*: a head buried in folded arms, in a somewhat sloppy yoga position, the new beggar (in the way one speaks of the new poor) is more fitting in the Latin Quarter (Odéon, Sèvres) than in the sixteenth arrondissement or working-class neighborhoods. Beggars "give something to look at," but offer nothing more than themselves, a brute presence, a massive absence; they "give something to look at" but look at no one, without the aid of sunglasses and white canes that are still found in the northern reaches of the metro, not blind at all, but without eyes, obvious, without words and without a job, a pure passivity, an unvoiced appeal interpellating only those who want to be "interpellated" and who, feeling themselves interpellated "somewhere," as has long been said in intellectual circles before beginning to measure the ridiculousness of an expression, give them alms for some obscure reason, maybe because they unconsciously consider the beggar to be like one of these people whom Mauss tells us are, in the eyes of others, "the representatives of the gods and the dead. . . . Alms are the result on the one hand of a moral idea about gifts and wealth and on the other an idea about sacrifice. Generosity is necessary because otherwise Nemesis will take vengeance upon the excessive wealth and happiness of the rich by giving to the poor and the gods."[11] God's share, poor people's share. A few years ago, some young people tried to attribute it to panhandling by turning every passerby into a symbol of happiness and wealth: "Ya got a buck?" But this provocation was carried out, like that of the cruiser, with the face exposed; at least it offered the more or less successful display (there again, a question of talent) of candor or of cynicism.

The obligation to give back in the case of beggars without voice or gaze is transformed into a pure obligation to give, the most important thing not being that few actually give, but that all or many feel, at least in passing, that when they do not give, they have to explain to themselves the reason that they did not. In these anonymous silhouettes, wild and ill-adapted flowers in a "French-style" society (as it is said of gardens), we recognize the limits and signs of our collective identity: these beggars are what we are not, proof that we share with others at least this negativity. They don't play, they no longer play the game by the rules we accept (juridical, artistic, economic . . .). All moorings broken and with their only link to the world the scribbled text at their feet (sometimes written directly on the ground), they symbolize by way of negation and to the point of dizziness the whole social order, terribly concrete and terribly complete— black holes in our daily galaxy.

That is probably one of the reasons for the sacred disquiet

they arouse. They are an insurmountable, impassable border, a bit like the living dead. And the idea of making an offering to zombies is part of an obvious and immediate desire to stay within our borders—neither anonymous panhandlers slumped on the cement floors of passageways nor even any of our accidental companions: neither emaciated artists, whom we might more easily picture in the attics of another century than in the labyrinth of a tunnel connecting subway stations where the echo of their talent resounds like a twinge of remorse, nor bums drunk on wine and fatigue, nor any of the people we brush against in the cars or corridors and whose age, sex, clothing, readings, and other details primarily show us how different they are from us.

Thus the ethnologist in the subway (the ethnologist of his or her own society, even if it involves only an occasional, circumstantial ethnology, a matter of killing time between two stops) faces the task of grasping every individuality as if it summed up all by itself the whole social order (if only because a certain number of external signs that have meaning only in a specific cultural and historical context allow its situation, its tastes, and its origins at least to be imagined), and that of putting to work, with regard to each of them, the "unlimited process of the objectivation of the subject" so dear to Lévi-Strauss; letting his or her gaze slip from the blind and almost mineral mass of the panhandlers in the passageways to the familiar silhouette of a colleague on the platform, by way of fantasy and reason the ethnologist can take the relative measure of all possible objectivities.

It will be probably be difficult for the ethnologist, even without leaving the station where he or she usually takes the metro, to construct a unique object from the sum of emotions, calculations, and interests that waiting for the next train represents at a given moment for each and all of the travelers, but these subjective and objective elements can never truly be totalized; never can a social fact be totally perceived in the way Lévi-Strauss understood it. Yet the subway spectacle offers us, more than others, the opportunity and the means to appreciate what can be perhaps not the typical personality of the user, but the totality of the entreaties of images and suggestions to which all users must react, if only to refuse them or to pretend to be unaware of them. For, whatever the originality of the responses or reactions, it is definitely measured according to the stereotypical character of this whole, which itself, as a kind of norm, sketches well an ideal image of the consumer, of the seductive woman, of the friendly young couple or the virile man, and about which it would be difficult to say if it is shaping reality or reflecting it.

This spectacle on the walls is seen not only in the tunnels or on subway platforms; it takes place on the street and yet again in the evening on television. But in the subway, whether as a model or a copy, I grasp it more closely, embodied in my daily neighbors, at the mere sight of whom I believe I can imagine their apartments, furniture, amusements, and even the next vote they will cast, or at least the reasons they will give for voting they way they did. I should add that these efforts of the imagination, independent of their inherent risk of error, in no way proceed from any kind of scorn, because I could never accomplish them if I did not feel close to those whom they take as an object, accessible to their reasons and permeable to their moods, to the point of sometimes only feeling, after the questions I ask myself about them, a kind of doubt about the exact nature of what separates us.

Correspondences

A lame devil in tunc with the century, who suddenly threw the entire Paris region out of gear, would discover a very strange arrangement, a gigantic social game, a labyrinth with countless exits, a somewhat decelerated scenic mechanism: several dozen levels in fact that are not only spread out in a network over the entire expanse of the urban and periurban zone, but also staggered on several levels, invaded at regular intervals by a more or less compact crowd of players of all kinds following the commands of a mysterious director, the god-architect of this subterranean universe.

His gaze, like our own, would at first be riveted by the meticulous interlacing of lines. Then perhaps, dreaming, in a cynical aside, of the probable uniformity of human solitude, he would contemplate for a moment, with the resigned indulgence of one of Homer's gods, as we have been tempted to do, the uncertain face of a given passenger imprisoned in her or her car. But he would probably be quickly drawn toward and retained by the teeming spectacle of the complicated knots that tie the lines to one another, knots of corridors and stairways with individuals coursing through them in every direction and giving the impression they know where they are going. "What can this correspond to?" he would wonder, by playing on the word *correspondance,* and, getting caught up in his game, he might add: "What does it correspond to to change every day, to start over again every day changing in order to take the same direction?"

But the ethnologist is suspicious of the view from Sirius; he or she knows that from too far away, everything loses its meaning, and that a cosmonaut eternally spinning in orbit, with no hope of return, would have as little interest in the earth as in the moon. The ethnologist dreams of intimacy and returns underground, even if he or she is not insensitive, now and then, especially if the weather is nice, to the mad impulse that pushes the subway into thinking it is airborne as it leaps over the Seine and speeds toward Étoile.

By way of parenthesis, these flights of fancy are disturbing from more than one point of view. First of all, they break up the intimacy of the underground trip; once beyond Sèvres-Lecourbe, everybody raises their nose and strikes a pose: neighbors become witnesses—a question of light, probably. When the trip takes a little longer than usual, the status of passengers changes somewhat; they are less tolerant of the gaze of others and dare less to look at them; voyeurism takes its distance: parallel to the tracks, however, the windows of the apartment buildings on the third and fourth floors are often closed and the curtains drawn, as if the happy inhabitants of these places were obliged to "play subway" at home and the whole day long to enjoy the quietude of a padded room in which the light is always on. Some people, more extroverted, more astute, or simply higher up, lean on their elbows at the window and watch the subways go by, the way others watch trains or cars from highway footbridges. Like my imaginary devil, they invert the perspective, profiting from the situation in order to observe the clearly transitory but always recurrent spectacle of the subway and human febrility. From inside the train, to be sure, those who are looking around with curiosity and who are not sacrificing to either reading or meditation, return their look and watching pass by the intimate snippets of private Parisian lives, the traffic jams along the thoroughfares of the fifteenth arrondissement, and the slow rush (for the difference in respective speeds creates the equivalent of a slow-motion effect) of those running to catch the subway at the next station.

They cannot make it, but: in the open air, the subway is a show, and the gaze of the strollers who do not wish to see in it the nocturnal strangeness that Godard was able to capture, lingers on it a bit with a friendly nonchalance, to the point that were it not for the crowd, the noise, the congestion of the streets, they would surely raise their arms—the way children sometimes still do when a train or cars go by—to wave hello or good-bye to those whom they will have as little occasion to see again as they did to see them in the first place—an astonishing and natural gesture, astonishingly natural, a gesture of hospitality without the time to be offered, pure sociability. Thus, a great deal of culture is needed to create something resembling a second state of nature and so that the products of human ingenuity can symbolize the great anthropological themes: identity, relation, destiny. Armand Camargue's quatrain in his *Croquis parisiens* [Parisian sketches] comes to mind:

> Il buvait un blanc sec au Canon de Grenelle
> En regardant passer les métros aériens.
> Le soleil par instants agaçait sa prunelle
> Il pensait à l'amour, à la mort, à des riens.

> [He was drinking a glass of chardonnay
> While watching the aerial subways in flight.

On his pupil often flickered the light of day
Before his mind love, death, and trifles were in sight.]

And also Charles Trenet, in "Y a de la joie" [We've got joy]:

Miracle: à Javel
On voit le métro qui sort de son tunnel.

[Miracle: at Javel
You can see the metro coming out of the tunnel.]

—even if this latter only approximates poetry.

Following our ethnologist underground, we now need to go from the metro symbol to the symbolic metro, that is, to the social practice of the metro insofar as it engages what Lévi-Strauss (in the text referred to earlier) calls "symbolic systems."

The reader will excuse me at this point for adopting a more didactic tone. Time and space are needed to move from one activity to another; that is what subway trips express, whose intensity is a function of the schedule of those who make them, because, in changing activity at certain hours they are also changing place. Now, these changes of activity are not simple technical changes; they can involve genuine changes of role, for example, when they correspond to a transition from what we call a professional life to one we call private. The opposition private life/professional life does not by itself account for all shifts of activity: there are more or less public forms of non-professional life (one might go, alone or with friends, to public places in search of entertainment, whether to the stadium, to parades, to fireworks displays, to the theater, or to the movies) and many forms of private life—official or secret, familial or solitary, legal, religious ... The spectacle of the subway has a similarly romantic character, especially in the tunnels connecting different lines that passengers use to change trains the way one changes a symbolic system and practice, changing life at regular hours, for lack of changing one's life (as they said in 1968), unless some "adventure" or particular event that is out of the ordinary draws them more clearly away from the beaten path and their usual lines.

A few subways are clearly more romantic than others: in the afternoon, at about three or four o'clock, when the ordinary mortal is in the office, workshop, factory, or school, the subways are not empty; encounters are possible that are less anonymous than during rush hour; and on occasion we can always wonder who the unknown man or woman who briefly caught our attention was and where they were going. Sometimes in *Libération* one can read somewhat silly yet very moving notices of young people who are discovering the cruel pleasures of the spirit of the stairway: "You were beautiful, brunette, and sweet; I was small, timid, and stupid; you were wearing a red blouse; I was seated next to you; you said "Excuse me" to me as you got off at Concorde. Do you remember?" Here again Perec's formula might be useful: how many minutes does it take to change one's life? It is a good guess, however, that the emotion of the *Libé* reader results especially from the disappearance of the woman he would like to see come back; he loves, he hates the movement that shifts the lines, the instant when, regaining his liberty, an elegant silhouette reveals the reality of his existence by disappearing—a person, a life, a body that are suddenly identified with the necessity of their itinerary.

Camargue again:

> Elle descend toujours à Sèvres-Babylone
> Et j'admire sa grâce indolente et félonne
> Quand pensive un instant elle marque le pas
> À l'angle du couloir de la correspondance
> Avant de s'élancer de sa marche qui danse
> Vers des plaisirs pervers que je ne connais pas.

> [She always gets off at Sèvres-Babylone
> And the lazy and felonious grace I admire is one
> When, pensive, for a moment she will advance

Toward the turn of the corridor of her correspondence
Before moving her feet with steps that dance
Toward perverse pleasures I fancy by chance.]

The reader will forgive this new digression and allow me to return to symbolic systems. We know that for Lévi-Strauss any
culture "can be considered as a combination of symbolic systems."[1] These systems, which express certain aspects of reality,
uphold various relations, whether of language itself, matrimonial rules, economic relations, art, science, or religion. They
nonetheless remain incommensurable, at once because each
system has its own rhythm of evolution and its specific vulnera-
bility when coming into contact with other cultures, and because, in any case, the respective symbolisms of each system
cannot be fully translated from the one to the other. A society is
thus comparable "to a universe in which only discrete masses
are highly structured."[2] Lévi-Strauss finally notes in this respect
that, on the one hand, the building of a comprehensive symbolic structure can be "achieved only on the level of social life," the
latter made clear in some way in its chronological deployment,
and, on the other hand, that in every society the task "of incar-
nating incompatible syntheses" has been assigned to individuals
placed outside of systems, such as the shaman or the man who
is possessed during certain ceremonies, but who are indispensable to the coherence of the total system, which, without them,
might risk "disintegrating into its local systems."[3]

What helps us to perceive the tunnels of the changes between subway lines is precisely the moment—impalpable and
uncertain, to be sure—in which ordinary citizens shift from one
system to another, the time of a trip that is outside of all systems, but shared among their warmest memories and their
freshest anticipations, possibly preoccupied by what they have
just left or what they are going to find, ready to change language
as they change location, ready and prepared, prepared for what
awaits them ("Get ready! You're going to be late!"), sometimes a
little tired, and enervated ("I lead a crazy life") when the her-

metic barriers that ought to assure the peace of household lives, individual happiness, or professional calm give way, just as, on another scale, other barriers claim to assure the division of labor, the separation of powers, or civil peace. Having no possible recourse to dances of possession or a shamanic vision, they are very aware that if these barriers were to give way, as they sometimes threaten to do, they would go crazy, and that preferable to this precipitation—in the chemical sense—of the discrete elements they deal with throughout the day is still the precipitation in the ordinary and trivial sense that makes them run after their various lives—but, after all, it's their life—from one end of the subway system to the other.

Thus, the theme of the total social fact confronts us with another impossible totality. Just as it is impossible to understand, imagine, or fully represent the sum of subjectivities that at once perceive it and enter into its composition, it is out of the question to conceive simultaneously the diversity of the moments and spaces that compose one of its raw materials. No practice (and this is a truism) can be understood in synchrony. But the metro's transfer points are one of the best places for an empirical (and partial) approach to the idea of the total social fact: both because anyone who travels through the maze (Theseus arrogantly sure of himself) can be stopped in flight between two trapezes, conjugating in his or her own way the verb "to change," and because any one of those who happen to be there at the same time, despite the regularity of the overall movements, is not at the same point of his or her itinerary (some are going home, others are leaving, still others are escaping)— whether the daily itinerary or the long-term one: the steep pitch of the stairways mercilessly reveals the inequality of bodies and ages. It is obvious that every day in the metro there are individuals who are taking their first trip and others their last.

Of course, no strategy of inquiry can be found here, even if, I believe, the subway corridors ought to provide a good "turf" for the apprentice ethnologist, if only he or she gives up interrogating those who use them (but not chatting with them if the opportunity arises), even worse *(horresco referens!)*, polling them, and is content to observe and listen to them, indeed, to follow them. The apprentice will probably run the risk of gathering clichés (understood here in a strictly photographic sense, as snapshots) and of getting lost in trying to arrange the kaleidoscopic images that at first sight appear arbitrary, disconnected, and baffling. The apprentice can try to classify them by genre; maybe then the resulting inventory will begin to take shape, in a promising way, with a little optimism and imagination: a thousand items recorded, a hundred possible poems, ten future novels—which corresponds to at least three vocations. But stubborn and determined to practice the ethnologist's tasks, the apprentice can then try other classifications, other crosschecks, and begin at the beginning.

The monograph of a large station with its change of lines, with a transfer point, would have to open with a methodical description of place; the monograph has always been an excellent ethnographic exercise, and probably the most difficult if attention is paid to the fact that the *monos* of monograph signifies totality as much as unity: a single but complete whole. Thus, first of all, one would have to draw up a schema indicating the level and location of each platform, clearly note the connections of the two-way or one-way corridors providing access to each one of them and passage from the one to the other, locate and situate exactly the main entry and the various other entries, as well as the windows where tickets and monthly passes are sold, assess the difficulty of access to different points of departure, the length of the corridors and stairways, and, where appropriate, the convenience of the escalators. I daresay this study of the natural milieu, or of physical morphology, is an indispensable prerequisite for whoever subsequently wants to assess more closely either the degree of habit on the part of certain travelers— the professionals, in a way, of this station—or the various difficulties encountered by others (improvisers, elderly persons, foreigners), or the sense of location and the positioning on the part of those offering certain artistic services, and, beyond that, the particular sociology of different lines, or rather, of different combinations of lines (tell me who you are listening to and I'll tell you what line you take).

But that is already tantamount to approaching a more qualitative aspect of ethnological work, assuming that all the useful deductions have been made (frequency of the trains and the degree of traffic at different times of the day and on different days of the week; average number of travelers going directly into the subway through the station, also at different times of the day and on different days of the week; possible account taken of department stores, large institutions, or educational establishments situated near the station). As for qualitative work properly speaking, it might be done in two directions.

In the station itself, on all the platforms and in every corridor, a list needs to be drawn up of all the posters that by various means seek to attract and hold the passerby's attention—an exact estimate can be made, moreover, following extensive and repeated observations, of the success these posters have with various sections of the public, which, furthermore, they are helping to define. We know that the advertising poster itself conforms to a particular rhythm. Complementary technological studies could be useful accompaniments to the monograph: the broad and precise gesture of people putting up posters is one of the last traditional gestures that can be observed in the capital, and I have always wondered how they do it without gluing themselves to the wall along with the posters they smear with paste. A first distinction would have to be made among posters that appear on a regular basis and that provide information about Parisian nightlife, in particular the theater (they have survived the Morris columns that are today being revived), those, of a much more recent vintage, aimed at launching a film and whose placement is sometimes original (it took me a moment to understand—or, rather, to see—that the two posters "Rive Droite" [Right Bank], "Rive Gauche" [Left Bank], each of which offered a very lovely view of Paris by night, were the advertisement for one and the same film, *Rive Droite, Rive Gauche*), and those, naturally, that assure a longer-lasting advertising campaign for a product or a company; the latter can play either on familiarity with their logo or their symbols (we recognize Mother Denis at first glance) or on a change of image; they can also play with time, creating a suspense of the type "next week I will take off my underwear" (which was not, this time, an underground event), to capture and hold the attention of a spectator who, unlike one in television or the movies, is a passerby.

What would remain would be to analyze the content of the posters and, first of all, to note the favored themes and forms in the metro compared to other advertising sites. We can presume that the essential difference has to do with the fixed character of subway images compared to the fleeting character of audio-visual images; this distinction nonetheless remains relative to the extent that, although it could be said that in the subway, in contrast to television, it is the viewer who moves and the image that stays put, it must be added that with the spectator-traveler coming back and passing by now and again, the two types of image probably draw a similar degree of effectiveness from their recurrent character; but one might also wonder if the specificity of images and ads in the subway does not depend on their underground character. The image of the subway, like that of weeklies, is rarely contemplated in a group; very frequently a singular, indeed fleeting and vaguely shameful, relationship is created along with it, a duplicitous relation of conniving sleaze that advertising, when it offers images of the body, puts under the aegis of aesthetics in order to absolve the viewer, while these images are immediately and intimately felt as an erotic provocation. Bearing witness to this provocative character are graffiti, inscriptions, obscene drawings that can comment on or sometimes retouch ads outrageously, cutting through feminine underwear whose "spidery" delicacy has visibly been perceived as an appeal to rape, just as "pulpy" mouths (it is hardly surprising that my adjectives here are all borrowed from drugstore literature), mouths that invite us to savor the taste of a chocolate or the quality of a lipstick, arouse among a few wild artists phantasms that can truly be called redundant. A more or less strongly registered, and more or less easily tolerated idea of the body and of its beauty spreads through advertisements for lingerie, swimsuits, or carbonated drinks: it would nonetheless be useful, in order to specify the exact degree of influence, if our ethnologist tried to observe the way different categories of individuals—in groups or alone, young or adult—react to the image, pay no attention to it, or comment on it, study it, or steal a more or less furtive glance at it.

We can remark parenthetically that if the apprentice's study of the turf, as would be desirable, were to extend over a period of several years, he or she would have every opportunity to observe significant changes, such as the one that (if we stick to the idea of the body) has resulted in the masculine body acceding to the dignity of an erotic object: underwear, eaux de cologne, jeans, or premium beers are henceforth shown, in images extolling their qualities, as revealing agents of the virility they symbolize. And because we are probably less accustomed to the image of the male as object than of the female as object, the advertising effect is, for that reason, more perceptible: it proceeds squarely from the fallacy that tends to make us admit that if a virile man is shown wearing a given brand of briefs or jeans, whoever wears them will also be virile. But this metonymic inversion could not work (by inciting men, or their wives, to buy briefs or jeans) if the mere juxtaposition of images, which involves on the part of the artist painter or photographer a very realistic sense of form and contour, did not involve our conviction, by an effect of contiguity that we qualify as magical when we encounter it among others.

The image of the body extends to the dimensions of an art of living and of an art of happiness when other themes are associated with it: Greece, Tunisia, and Morocco with their sunshine; self-confidence and the very calm maturity it seems to promise to massive adults like American actors; the standard houses that guarantee health and prosperity against a background of green lawns stage, in the garden, a resplendent and healthy body whose most intimate representations express rather, in the courtyard, a capacity for pleasure and desire. It is unquestionably true that the subway has no monopoly on either these images or these themes, that it is not the only place where, if not a "vision of the world," at least an image of the individual and of life is spread. But it is also obvious, on the one hand, that these images derive a particular force from accompanying every day, underground, all those people whose trip isolates them just long enough to make them pass from one form of sociability to another, and, on the other hand, that the very nature of these images (svelte and desirable bodies, to be sure, but even more, expressive bodies, state-of-soul bodies, attitudes, movements, looks) must especially be taken into consideration at a time when the omnipresent sin is anthropomorphism and the endless creation of historical Subjects (Mr. Capital and Mrs. Earth lead difficult lives), and whose entire imagery and chattiness tend to suggest that the truth of being resides in appearance: What is the *form* of the president? What is the *state* of opinion, the *health* of the enterprise?

As in the societies whose study ethnography has long favored, because it believed them to be different from our own, we are now increasingly sensitive to the appearance of beings and things, the only thing capable of making sense of things— to tone of voice more than content of the discourse, to determining the gaze more than thought, to the look, to the "punch," to the jawbone. From this point of view, everybody discovers in the subway—in short, as in the proverbial Spanish inn—what they bring to it (repugnance or fascination and, more generally, a subtle combination of the two) and, at the same time, a kind of objective confirmation of the reality of the surrounding world and of the values that are so spectacularly displayed in it: the image never stops proving the image.

This play of images defines the universe everyone frequents and shares. But the ethnologist, like everyone else, realizes that an undifferentiated social universe cannot exist and that values, like everything else, are not equally shared. The qualitative work of the ethnologist therefore ought to explore a second line and, in the given instance, the sum of the lines with which his or her station is connected. For the geography of the neighborhoods is not that of the stations, and the most luxurious of neighborhoods are often frequented during the day by people who work there but do not live there. Thus Franklin D. Roosevelt is a popular station where large numbers of employees, lower-level managers, and secretaries get on and off. And it is a good guess that on the upper level of the station (the upper level alone, for a certain number of those who walk through it never go down the stairs), many people cross paths but never meet.

Many interesting observations could still be made in this respect in the station or its environs; our ethnologist might thus notice that, little by little, different businesses are setting up shop, officially or stealthily, in this intersection known as a *correspondance,* and dream of the progressive sacralization of a place in which are concentrated all the composite parts and all the allegories of the modern world (the press and current events, business and style, advertising and the ideals that it relays and fashions, the public function behind the counters, the law and its representations—more visible at République than at Franklin D. Roosevelt, perhaps—and also youth, work, vacations on the horizon—posted on the walls like a promise: the foreigner, the tourist, or the immigrant). Have not the places of this genre (public square, market, intersection) been places of worship in all civilizations? To what Hermes are we sacrificing ourselves? Perhaps then, depending on the mood of the moment, the ethnologist might be inclined to think that the abstract silhouette of the faceless beggar or the enthusiasm of the unknown musician represents, at this intersection of human fates, the presence of the god to whom alms are given so that life can continue. Or, in a prosaic but no less Durkheimian way—optimistic and secular to the point of enthusiasm—he or she might consider that the existence of an intersection without gods, without passions, and without battles these days represents the most advanced stage of society and prefigures the ideal of all democracies.

It would remain for the apprentice ethnologist to change his or her point of view by leaving the studied station in order to follow—as a cop, a lover, an onlooker—a few of those whose itinerary until then had only been imagined or reconstructed. Perhaps, with a great deal of patience and talent, the ethnologist might then succeed, by dint of multiplying descriptions, in retracing paths, understanding ways of doing things, experiencing or exhausting feelings and affect, in sketching for modernity what Oscar Lewis had accomplished for poverty: the fragile but living portrait, perhaps more real than true, of a "culture," that is, of everything by which each person feels both like others and different from them—but not so different that, with respect to other others, he or she does not irrevocably express solidarity.

Conclusions

On the Subway in General

Métro, boulot, dodo [subway, job, sleep]: only a somewhat lazy irony could contest this triad as a symbol of modern alienation. The constraints it reflects are those of all social life; one might even, continuing along this line of thought, note that the somewhat inverted negative of the sequence (no more work, no more subway, no more sleep) would be a better symbol for the difficulties of the time, by making free hours and insomnia a result of unemployment. Subway, job, sleep: the interesting thing is, to the contrary, to understand how the sense of individual life is born of the global constraints that apply to all social life. Except for a few cultural details and a few technological adjustments, every society has its subway, and imposes on each and every individual itineraries in which the person uniquely experiences how he or she relates to others. That the sense is born of alienation has long been shown by ethnology, among other disciplines, and this truth remains paradoxical only because a certain idea of the individual resists it, anchored in the sensitive evidence of the body, which, in turn and return, defines the limits and meaning of the social.

On the Parisian Metro in Particular

When I was in high school, our French teacher pointed out to us that the most beautiful Alexandrine in the French language was printed on the windows of the doors of subway cars. A few years ago still, in fact (because this inscription in its original formulation has since disappeared), the R.A.T.P. used to explain in these terms the meaning of its interdictions:

> "Le train ne peut partir que les portes fermées."

> [The train can only leave if the doors are closed.]

The Racinian perfection of this Alexandrine, on which the mute *e* imprinted an extended vibration, enthralled our professor, who was much less satisfied with its sequel, despite its exquisitely urban tone, because of the incongruous placement of its caesura and because, despite its final feminine syllable, it did not rhyme with the one that preceded it:

> "Prière de ne pas gêner leur fermeture."

> [Please do not impede their closing.]

In the same breath he explicated Pascal for us ("We're all aboard") in such a way that the image of the Parisian metro for me has always been associated with the ineluctable and irreversible character of the individual human voyage; that was the year of classical tragedy and of Jansenism: the eighteeenth century still lay ahead of me in the junior year, and the nineteenth awaited the final year of school. But already the metro had taught that one can always change lines and stations, and the fact that if one can't escape the labyrinth of the network, it at least offers some beautiful detours.

Afterword: Riding the Subway with Marc Augé
Tom Conley

I

Much of what Marc Augé develops in *In the Metro* is shaped in the second and third chapters of *La Traversée du Luxembourg*, a blueprint for many of the books Augé has since written over the past two decades. The form of *La Traversée du Luxembourg* betrays a desire to wrestle free of the tradition of a monograph while retaining the fruits of its style of investigation. Like Claude Lévi-Strauss before him, the master ethnographer who wrote the groundbreaking *Elementary Structures of Kinship* (1949) before completing *Tristes Tropiques* (1955), Augé wants to be both a writer and a scientist. Whereas Lévi-Strauss cribbed some of the chapters of his first published dissertation, *La Vie familiale et*

sociale des Nambikwara (1948), by editing (even censoring) and
pasting them directly into the most poetic chapters of *Tristes
Tropiques,* in *La Traversée du Luxembourg* Augé produces a work
that might be called a critical autobiography. It lacks a table of
contents but is sectioned into eight chapters that an allegorist
would calculate to be each of the working hours of the author's
day. At 7 A.M. the author wakes up to the news of his clock radio,
learns who is leading the Tour de France, the weather forecast
for the day, and the future of the prime minister, Laurent Fabius,
in his campaign to gain leadership of the Socialist Party. "A few
catastrophes in the Orient escape my ears when, turning back on
my right side, I stretch out and risk putting an uncertain foot on
the floor to the right of the bed (an old habit, the story, surely, of
not getting up on the wrong side of the bed), I go about the task
of heating a little coffee in the kitchen."[1] When the warm elixir
soothes his throat, he is reminded of a lingering soreness. The
eighth and final chapter of the novel takes place in the late afternoon, when he leaves the office of the doctor, who assures him
that the pain he felt in the morning and throughout the day is no
cause for worry. He is, he mentions, "happy." The book he has
just finished avers to be a *practice* of happiness for the reason
that the craft of style and its many pleasures and resistances have
been put to good work.

In the final pages, he ruminates about a lecture he will soon
deliver in Palermo. He remembers he needs to retrieve a note-
book at his apartment before going to the airport. He is observing the company at the Closerie des Lilas (near the Port-Royal
metro stop). While he muses, he sees them dining through the
shrubbery surrounding the terrace. They are in "the happiness
of the moment." Time presses. "I'm going to take a taxi. I'm
happy" (196). Between the beginning and the end of the day,
when he convinces himself in view of the crowd at the Closerie,
yes, that he *is* happy, Augé reflects on a multitude of things. His
thoughts seem to move errantly, like the sentences of Marcel
Proust's *In Search of Lost Time.* Their origins return, like the
afterthought of a scholar, to document a train of thought that

would have preferred to be free of footnotes. At the close of the first chapter, thoughts about leisure and work are substantiated by allusion to Georges Bataille's *Accursed Share*. Then divagations on suburban space and the gap between generations are sustained by references to Georges Balandier, Lévi-Strauss, and Émile Durkheim. An encounter with a nervously voluble friend engages reflections on neorural communities in central France, a product of some of the utopian illusions of 1968, the topic of work engaged with Dominique Léger. The sixth chapter, on religious revival, is built from the author's own article on the topic written for the *Encyclopaedia Universalis*. A long account about structure and myth in telenovels—especially *Dallas*—is crafted from Augé's earlier account in *Le Temps de la réflexion*. Then a chapter treating sports in everyday life is written as a critical reading of Allen Guttman's *From Ritual to Record,* a book of 1977 that decries the professionalization of athletics in America. In its sum, the book offers a chronicle and a program of research swaying between research in Africa, dialogue with canonical texts of ethnography, and life on a summer day in Paris.

The reader finds neither allusion to the grandfather of everyday life, Henri Lefebvre, nor fellow travelers Guy Debord and the Situationists, nor even reference to Michel de Certeau, the proponent of "spatial stories" in Paris told in *The Practice of Everyday Life.* Augé stakes his fiction on how an account of a day of travel in the city can be of import to anthropology. He implies that in the age of "supermodernity" (a substantive that will become the subtitle of his *Non-lieux* treating of the effects of multinational capitalism) the stakes of studying "traditional" cultures defined by isolation or by being "without history" need revision. Mix and confusion of peoples have been constant throughout human time, and so why not draw the talents of the fieldworker into the dilemmas of the city and the nation at large? Why not extend the limits of sociology by looking at quotidian life through a lens of partial (as opposed to Mauss's overarching vision of total) social facts? These questions inform *La Traversée du Luxembourg,* but most pertinently its few pages devoted to life in the subway, which become the germ of his terse reflections in *In the Metro*.

They are worth reviewing. Chapter 3 begins at the Sèvres-Babylone station, "my daily intersection" (61), where every day he arrives, hustles through the corridors, and changes trains without giving much thought to what he is doing there. The station links the space of home and work, but it is not quite a site of what Lefebvre called "mediated" or lost time because the passage affords Augé reflection on the unspoken and secret pleasures of riding the train:

> The subway is a soft drug. But it's a drug of luxury because time is required to appreciate its real value. But not necessarily a great deal of time, but staggered time, the time that others spend for work, for eating or sleeping, to reproduce the requirements of work that will thrust them into the station at rush hour. The consumer of staggered time, of the time made by the hours that the National Railway or the Postal Service call "hollow," does not envision the underside, as might a seer or a shaman of exotic cultures, but the traveler sometimes glimpses its surface, which in the urban universe is much more difficult. Rarely does a Parisian visit Paris, and rarely do we spare a glance at the buildings we work in, or even the edifices that eventually turn our itineraries into landscapes in the eyes of the tourist who discovers them. (63)

The difference leads Augé to superimpose the plan of the Parker Brothers' *Monopoly* board game onto the map of the subway. The move is related to shifts from one "symbolic system" to another, and is quickly exemplified in the transfer that riders make from one subway line to another. A culture, which Lévi-Strauss defines as the aggregate of symbolic systems, is likened to the thirteen (and, since 1999, fourteen) lines that riddle the map of Paris. He observes that, in order to arrive at the definition, Lévi-Strauss began by taking a "Marx-Language" line before crossing over to a "Lacan-Symbolic Theory" line where it was easier to see one's relation with oneself and others. Herein the refrain of *In the Metro* begun in *La Traversée du Luxembourg*: "Every individual life, because it is social before the young child has ever opened its mouth (that won't change a thing) . . . is essentially alienated; unique, however, unique as every one of my neighbors in the subway car, but condemned to follow or to believe they are inventing itineraries with social significance" (71). The point of transfer in the station, the *carrefour*, becomes the point where the individual and collective dimensions of a society find a point of correspondence. At the end of the chapter, he dreams of an African divinity, Legba, sculpted over doorways, at the marketplace, and at intersections of the metro. Avatar of Hermes, Legba would receive sacrifices made where lines are changed at Sèvres-Babylone.

Like the lingering cough, the dilemma of generalizing an account of a day in the life of a professor of anthropology requires a careful negotiation of documentation and narcissism. The reader of *In the Metro* senses that Augé revises speculation on the "self" begun in *La Traversée du Luxembourg*. The Parisian metro, taken from its definition as a metaphor and, possibly, a "total social object" in the earlier work, now becomes a place in which secrets are circulating. Autobiographical snippets are cut through the book, but they indicate little about how and why the author descends into the metro—perhaps because of a wound of either personal or historical origin, of a solitude that cannot be put into words, or even, as many sentences suggest, by reason of the ineffable quality of everyday life in an urban setting. The fuzziness of a secret is glimpsed in the first sentence, where a childhood memory invokes a troubled relation— both individual and collective—with an unnamed event in the author's lifetime that grounds reflections on structure, literary allegory, and the beginnings of subjectivity. "The first German soldier I remember seeing was at Maubert-Mutualité in 1940, upon return from the exodus. Until then the Germans had only been an immaterial and diffuse presence imposing endless shifts and revisions on our itinerary." An unnamed subway stop at the crossing of the boulevard Saint-Germain and the rue Monge, not a *station de correspondance,* locates the blur of memory. The place-name that the reader supplies situates the imaginary square of an individual's early impressions on a subway map. As a child the author had been evacuated from his origin prior to occupying it. Its very name, its *mot,* motivates myriad connections (Albertus Magnus, the "mutual" character of French and German citizens over the course of time) that do not seem to lead anywhere, neither to an allegory nor to the next station (Cluny-Sorbonne or Cardinal Lemoine). A collective itinerary, that might be one of evacuation, blends into another, that of the subway map, an icon of collective life in France since the nineteenth century.

Individual and collective fantasies are mixed from the word *go.* For readers familiar with the oeuvre, the same recollection is brought forward to color the author's earliest childhood memories, "not steeped in pigment, but rather a somewhat faded aquarelle where the vague colors of a seaside would lazily bite into each other." These are the tones, recounted in *Domaines et châteaux,* that are quasi-identical to those we find in *In the Metro.* In *Domaines et châteaux* he continues his recollection:

> The exodus: others knew it more dramatically. However uncertain the memories I retain, they impressed my memory. The road that we had to take at night, after several days of calm in the flatlands of Champagné, was for me only a long chaotic sleep punctuated by fleeting awakenings—stopovers marked by the flash of electric lamps and hurried words that were loudly exchanged with the police. The Loire: the word returned constantly. The Loire, a border, which we doubted and feared we would soon be crossing, was, in my mother's suspicion, located at the exact point where my father was in his retreat, and the enemy in its advance. The Pyrénées (a few days must have passed): I awaken in a room bathed

in sunshine; for the first time in my life I see mountains. The retreat is over. We've arrived. Soon we'll be back home.[2]

And so extends a relation with Proust, the memory of many sentences in *À la recherche du temps perdu* seemingly charting the course of the book. "Longtemps, pour moi, l'inconnu avait commencé à Duroc, début d'une série de noms dont je ne retenais que le terme, Porte d'Auteuil, parce que nous y descendions parfois le dimanche pour aller au bois" (For a long time, for me the unknown had begun at Duroc, the beginning of a series of names of which the last was the only one I could recall—Porte d'Auteuil, because we occasionally got off there on Sundays to walk to the park): this sentence echoes "Longtemps je me suis couché de bonne heure" (For a long time I went to bed early), the beginning of Proust's novel; at the same time it renews the narrator's struggles to gain an arbitrary relation with names. Proust's train of memory, which chugged along the coasts of Normandy and Brittany, will roll on the rails of Augé's metro:

Si ma santé s'affermissait et que mes parents me permissent, sinon d'aller séjourner à Balbec, du moins de prendre une fois, pour faire connaissance avec l'architecture et les paysages de la Normandie ou de la Bretagne, ce train d'une heure vingt-deux dans lequel j'étais monté tant de fois en imagination, j'aurais voulu m'arrêter de préférence dans les villes les plus belles; mais j'avais beau les comparer, comment choisir, plus qu'entre des êtres individuels qui ne sont pas interchangeables, entre Bayeux si haute dans sa noble dentelle rougeâtre et dont le faîte était illuminé par le vieil or de sa dernière syllabe; Vitré dont l'accent aigu losangeait de bois noir le vitrage ancien; le doux Lamballe qui, dans son blanc, va du jaune coquille d'œuf au gris perle; Coutances, cathédrale normande, que sa diphtongue finale, grasse et jaunissante, couronne par une tour de beurre.[3]

[Were my health strengthened and my parents willing, if not to go and sojourn at Balbec, at least take for one time, to gain a sense of the architecture and the landscapes of Brittany or Normandy, the 1:22 A.M. train in which I had so often traveled in my imagination, I would have wished preferably to stop in the most beautiful cities; but I had compared them fruitlessly, for how to choose, more than between individuals who are not interchangeable, between mighty Bayeux with its noble reddish lace and whose roof was illuminated by the immortal gold of its last syllable; Vitré, whose acute accent spliced a strip of black wood in its gothic glass; soft Lamballe that, in its white, goes from egg-yolk yellow to pearl grey; Coutances, a Norman cathedral that its last diphthong, fat and yellowing, crowns with a tower of butter.]

Proust here recalls the seasonal trains that carried tourists to cities and towns not yet accessible to automobiles. In the dark compartment of a night train he constructs a map that the novel continually revises to produce endless deformation and to draw forward things unknown.[4] The names and places of a thematic chart of Anglo-Norman and Breton gothic treasures is confused and rearranged (in the last clause above the cathedral church of Coutances, at whose crossing of the transept and the nave stands the greatest of all Anglo-Norman lantern towers, being suddenly coiffed with the analogous "Butter Tower" attached to the cathedral of Rouen, so named because a tax on butter was levied in 1484 to pay for its construction). Words and things can be mixed in lieu of individuals, he avows, who are inalterable, but who are forgotten in the dazzle of comparison. Optical aberration and a synesthesia of the times and spaces both past and present in *À la recherche* invite parallel reflection about what happens at the beginning of Augé's work.

The experience of most readers would no doubt confirm that the affinity broadens the scope of Augé's inquiry. If, as he suggested in the early pages of *La Traversée du Luxembourg,* a daily grind is framed by subway rides to and from work, the time spent inside the metro is cause for reflection on the way the days and years of our lives are lost in the train. Henri Lefebvre conceived the hours spent in transit to be those signaling the degree to which our bodies are wasted in a production of needless commodities in a regnum of "constrained time." Most histories of the subway strive to show that its engineers have worked to make travel efficient and cost-effective. Theirs is a search for time gained: at its beginnings, designers tried to assure smooth and efficient circulation of people within the core of the city, but with the growth of a population residing away from the workplace, travel to and from the centers and peripheries of Paris required revision and addition of lines in accord with a plan of center and circumference.[5] A dehumanization, a programmed alienation, gave rise to a consciousness of an *apparatus* bearing an ideology not just of transport, but also of what Louis Althusser outlined in 1968. The subway, like the school or the factory assembly line, the church or the movie theater, eventually emblematized the narcosis of life lived within a symbolic triangle defined by *métro, boulot, dodo* (subway, job, sleep).[6] This way of reading the history of the metro recurs in Augé's conclusions, where he argues, first, that in the years between 1968 and 1985 witnessing dramatic rises in unemployment, the absence of a subway would have been an even greater indication of malaise. Second, every reflection about what defines the subway, its place in daily life, and how it is used arches back to a "total metropolitan fact" concerning the meaning and direction of individual lives that are probably determined by rapid transit and public conveyances. We are all in the same train, but our reasons for being there are myriad and are also the result of infrastructural causes that would seem to have the subway as their fitting spatial emblem.

At the end of the book, poetry mediates the contradiction. The chance occurrence of an Alexandrine printed on the door, "Le train ne peut partir que les portes fermées" (The train can only leave if the doors are closed), makes literature mediate the passage of bodies. Augé recalls his first year in high school, when a professor taught the sublimities of French prosody through a common example. The memory gives way to reflection on the image that the subway has been for him: it is a social space in which are at play the chance and destiny of individual lives. The Alexandrine belongs to classical tragedy retrieved through the filter of the memories of high school. The writing stenciled on the door of the car affirms that a mental map or an inner cartographic image conveyed the same sense of play and fate that Augé would discover along the Ivory Coast. At the beginning, it is cartography, a variant of literary memory, that fashions the reflection. Hence, from the outset a relation is established between the total metropolitan fact to the subway map. "To speak of the metro first of all means to speak of reading and of cartography." The paragraph that follows this sentence early in the first chapter extends further some lines of the memory about names and places. Recalled are classrooms decorated with thematic wall maps, but also loci filled with memory sites from the "historical atlases" that students were asked to learn by heart. Augé cannot resist confusing the loose grid of the Parisian subway plan, a projection rivaling the standard map of France for prominence in the memory of all French citizens, with the spatial "takes" of great moments of national history. He calls the confusion "something of an accordion effect" wherein life, map, and official chronicle are overlaid. The reflection of the paragraph pauses, slanting away from personal memoir, by underscoring that where other thematic maps—of geology, agriculture, and the industries of France—ought to intervene in his meditation, so too should a stratigraphic means of reading them. The paradox is that the maps are cast into a parenthetical *aparté* (a space usually reserved for the irruption of emotion, adumbration, digression, or contestation), but in the affective slot is a Cartesian ordering revealing how Augé is classifying and gridding "amorous life, professional life, family life." The ellipsis promises the addition of terms that will eventually break the symmetry of the symbolic triangle of love, vocation, and

kinship. Further, the effect of suspension at the end of the enu-
meration bridges the labor of the ethnographer with that of the
novelist or poet.

The memorial form of *In the Metro* elegantly betrays the
stakes of an enterprise that ties the topological dimensions of
psychoanalytic anthropology that Augé had developed in work
on sorcery to the art of fiction. Unlike *La Traversée du Luxembourg,* which begins when the author gets out of bed on the
wrong foot, *In the Metro* starts with an antediluvian flash,
the memory of a grey specter retained because, inexplicably, the
name of a subway stop becomes the legend of the memory
image. The map and the toponyms of the Paris subway develop
into a webbing that holds and shapes events in the author's past
and even bears resemblance to patterns of lineage. He discerns,
like the dots adjacent to the names printed in red ink over the
fabulous detail of buildings and streets on most subway maps,
points of crossover and intersection. They are the thematic chi-
asms, Freudian "switch-words" that both mark junctures and
turn the wheels of memory in the mental machinery of everyone who descends into the metro. The subway map of Paris is located on a plane floating between irrefragable statistics concerning the structure and history of France (geology, agriculture,
industry), in which the biological body of any inhabitant plays a
minuscule role, and the individual, whose affect, whose diurnal
duties, and social life are invested in the cartographic plan.

Thus some "hinge dates" *(dates charnières)* in a person's life
become historical concretions, scars, or affective points confused with the red circles dotting the lines of the R.A.T.P. The
city dweller old enough to harbor memories of his or her past
will not fail to identify, sort through, and spatialize each image
through association with the place-names. So, along with the
recall of the thousands of thematic maps that edified the pupil in
the classrooms of childhood (for the postwar American, above
blackboards, the orange, blue, green, and brown wall maps
on wooden scrolls that bore the name of Denoyer-Geppert),
mapped images ultimately show the person how little his or her

life means in the geology of time. But in the same cartographic space are concealed intensely affective moments accessible only to the person glancing at the map while running to catch a train or dash out of an exit. "It would probably be possible, just as one analyzes the different periods of a painter's life (blue or pink, figurative or abstract . . .), to demarcate in the lives of many Parisians' successive 'periods,' such as a Montparnasse period, a Saint-Michel period, and a Bonne-Nouvelle period. Each of them (we know well) would surely correspond to a more secret geography: the subway map is also the Carte du Tendre or the open hand that one has to know how to fold and study closely in order to blaze a trail from the lifeline to the headline onto the heartline."

The practically unrivaled efficiency of the Parisian metro map is suddenly distorted through reminiscence.[7] But, as *La Traversée du Luxembourg* predicted, the itinerary moves toward and away from a central paradox, in which the pluralities of cultures before the anthropologist's gaze are different from, but never entirely foreign or strange to, each other. Each subway rider, too, discovers that his or her daily journey is unlike any other, including those of the traveler in his or her past, but that it resembles to a T so many that consume the minutes and hours of a lifetime. Entering the fray are the figures of difference and repetition, of reiteration, routine, habit, and listless drift. A continuum of torpor serves as the vital background for thoughts on cultures and total social facts that the rider may cogitate between one stop and the next. In the Parisian subway, sight, so common and quotidian, seems to make invisible the people of myriad origin, dress, ways of walking, idiom, intention, color, and demeanor before the somnolent rider's eyes.

To philosophize is to learn how to ride the subway. The boredom that we often see in the face of "other" subway riders would have the nearest equivalent to the point of departure of Lévi-Strauss's *Tristes Tropiques*. The other is routine, and so is anthropology. "Adventure plays no part in the profession of the ethnographer," he announced, noting that the fieldworker whit-

tles away hours and days of a lifetime in waiting for what—
somewhat like the train following the one the impatient traveler
has just missed—never comes. The native informant whom the
ethnographer shadows for days on end never really betrays
signs revealing the quirks of kinship or a truth about hierar-
chies of local space. In the routine of the subway, by contrast,
what seemed to be the end of kinship and the end of difference
is quickly displayed. The sight of the sheer mass and number of
cultural signs in the underground defies the observer. The final
evidence of variety, of motley multiculture, of paisley dapples of
difference is stuffed in the subway cars at rush hour. For the
subway rider who carries into the R.A.T.P. a copy of *In the Metro*
or *Tristes Tropiques,* the ends of cultures and time are momen-
tarily deferred when the book is read on the platforms or in the
moving cars.

Augé's image of the lifeline and the metropolitan *mappa
mundi* has uncanny parallels for the North American partisan
of the metro. In the subway of Washington, D.C., cavernous ex-
panses under basket-handle vaults of concrete caissons humble
the traveler at the Faneuil crossing. The blue, green, and yellow
colors of their respective lines on the map seem like chromatic
Velveeta homogenizing the class conflict embodied by the mix
of black and white subway riders, alternately in business suits or
jeans, basketball jerseys, and jogging togs, everyone standing in
cars designed for the space age. The spectacle is a far cry from
the jagged splashes of colors printed on the fabrics central Africans wear when they amble along the street from Barbès-
Rochechouart to Clignancourt. Or the Yankee grays and blacks
worn by denizens going to south Manhattan on the IRT, recalling the limited palette of Andrew Wyeth's paintings, darken the
fire-engine red paint glued, like oil-based mucilage, on the
I-beams and rivets of the girders at the Fourteenth Street and
Forty-second Street stations. The scene contrasts the speckles of
turquoise tickets littering the asphalt beneath garish posters on
the walls at any of the main exits from Montparnasse-Bienvenüe.
In Chicago, the contrast of black fans, who descend from the

elevated at Thirty-fifth and Shields on the way to Comiskey Park, is a strong contrast to the corporate types who throng at the Howard line en route to Wrigley Field. The image of crowds of every color chattering en route to soccer matches at the Stade de France is a study in flesh tones ranging from indigo to lily. At Park Street, the so-called melting pot of colors and cultures of Boston, the crossing where the red and green lines meet, "quaint" trolleys of one or two cars squeak and squeal through the station with agonizing deliberation. Inside, the bodies and idioms are distinguished: tanned Portos and Hispanics, ecstatic over the Pedro Martinez, ride by Kenmore Square, blending with ubiquitous Irishmen, their lily-white pallor and cheeks blushed with the rouge left by many glasses of Paddy's, while they bicker over Red Sox "shahtstahp Omah Gahciapahrer."

The sensorium of Augé's metro, a mix of delight and miasma, can extend to rapid transit in other metropolitan centers. Perhaps by way of the poetry he finds in the social facts of the underground, Augé, like Proust who led the way, subversively invites the reader to become an anthropologist for lack of available travel or means to get to exotic places that in reality exist only in the advertisements on the walls of the stations. A new ethnology begins when the "other" is diffused in any and every city. Fieldwork thus begins not far from home. The Paris Augé investigates is accessible for not much more than a dollar. The subway, as General Motors said in advertisements for the Chevrolet Bel Air in the 1950s, would offer a "pleasure in the going." It leaves for tourists the antique charm of the hydraulic levitation of elevators at the Eiffel Tower, or the crushing impact, felt in the *grande salle* of the Louvre, of Géricault's *Raft of the Medusa* floating away from the spectator. The subway offers wealth for the five senses, whether or not the major museums are closed or on strike. Yet the reader of *In the Metro* grasps an uneasy but telling relation between the tourist and the scientist of the ends of humanity. Avatar of the fabled protagonists of Balzac's novels about the perils of sentimental education in Paris—Raphaël of *The Wild Ass's Skin* or Lucien of *Lost Illusions*—the anthropolo-

gist discovers in the subway not only the postindustrial counterpart to timeless symbolic systems, but also a presence of isolation and solitude.

The Parisian traveler notes first and foremost a proximity of
the underground and the surface. The metro is built only several meters below the pavement, and thus the atmosphere
under the horizon of Paris (immediate because city codes usually forbid construction of buildings taller than five stories)
seeps into the air pushed through the stops as the trains enter
and exit. A commanding view of the volume of each station is
enhanced by the barrel vaults that make platforms seem compact. People are visible everywhere in the naves of Monge or
the catacombs of Denfert-Rochereau. The intrepid amateur of
things French, the economic traveler who invests exotic meaning in every impression and every object in the subway, is forever tempted to glimpse in the longitudinal sweep of the vault
a secular version of the central aisle of Notre-Dame. A Hugolian
antithesis, perhaps, of things beastly and beautiful is latent for
the reader of literature who rides the metro: the imagination
inhabits the church and the Cour des Miracles, where the "revival" of the gothic city in Viollet-le-Duc's filigree reconstruc-
tion finds its underbelly in the subway stop.

The stained-glass windows on the side aisles of the former
would be the gigantic posters on the walls of the latter, where
they wait to be read and, in the time of a casual glance, deci-
phered. The format of these advertising windows, of far greater
size than those on the walls of American subways, is so immense that their compositions begin to rival the serigraphies of
Roy Lichtenstein—for which tourists pay dearly in almost any
American museum of modern art. On the subway poster, the
subliminal seduction that is written into the ice cubes cooling
the fluid essence in a tumbler, or on the pouting lips of grouper-
like mannequins thrust in the faces of travelers, the fingers of
the models slipping between their skin and their jeans as if they
were preparing to gratify themselves at the handsome sight of
the spectator before their eyes, becomes refreshingly obvious.

Travelers who glimpse the recurring image of a single and same poster—say, in the endless corridor of Montparnasse-Bienvenüe, served by an equally endless "rolling carpet," a moving walkway to assist travelers moving between lines 13, 4, 12, and 6—sigh with relief when Jean Baudrillard's tired descriptive about things modern, "simulacrum," comes to mind, to be reminded that the rhetoric of baiting depends on serial repetition.[8] From stained glass above to the poster below, the ocular distance seems minimal, and so too the gap between things spiritual and temporal.

For the American rider, the displacement of the history and space of Paris above into the metro below is more than the effect of *flânerie* or eager synesthesia. It is more than the result of a Francophile's efforts to feel totalities of French culture and its evolutions in tessellations of rails and corridors beneath the city. An industrial mycelium replaces the symbiotic patterns of roots and rhizomes in the disappearing world of nature. A rider-tourist, his or her imagination imbued with the Frenchness of the French subway, senses how there prevails a mediation of rational planning, publicity, and imagination. Now and again the rider passes through stations that herald the history of their edification. Such, first, is the Louvre on the east–west line, where Augé notes how the bewildering charm expressed by foreign visitors in passing inspired him and other Parisians to realize that all of a sudden they became *staffage* in the cultural picture everyone was admiring. At the station, the presence of the foreign groups caused the natives of Paris to rediscover the "historical aura" that was assigning them preordained decorative roles.

The same stop reveals the history of the production of that aura. It dislodges a sensibility that identifies with the intellectual and optical pleasure of meeting both natives and tourists. At the Louvre stop, photographic enlargements and more "simulacra" of the treasures of the museum are seen in places otherwise reserved for posters. The design counts among André Malraux's first embodiments of the "imaginary museum" in postwar Paris. In the early 1970s, Parisians boasted that it sufficed to ride through the station instead of getting fatigued in the museum, or finding in the Louvre the rush-hour conditions of the subway in the room where foreigners flock around the Mona Lisa. The Louvre was suddenly simulated in the subway: if only—then felt this youthful Francophile listening to Parisians' gently ironic praise of the design that bespoke admiration ("What a treat!") and laziness ("We don't have to go upstairs anymore!")— Malraux were to thread the subway through the corridors of the palace in the way that a transparent plastic worm had recently burrowed through Lascaux, in order to preserve the cave from the corrosive contact of humans and their exhalations. A subway through the Louvre would be, as the new station suggested, the ultimate cinematography of art.[9]

Our meditations on the metro easily carry over to the New York subway. Unfamiliar with the French traditions of city planning that make art the necessity of invention, the rider in New York knows stations by the mosaic craft of wall signs displaying the number of the street. Art is caught in the minuscule lapse of time witnessed in the difference between the sights of the sans-serif character of the number printed on plates riveted to the I-beam struts of the platform and the older mosaic of cartouches high on the wall above and behind. The shape of the latter seems to mark what New Yorkers might call "our prewar years" that existed before the subway acquired its Taylorized look. Two ages, two times of life, are coextensive in the difference of printed characters. Thus the passenger sees how an older sense of duration inhabits the local lines. For the adept of the old East Side IRT, the anomaly of a train that stops at Fourteenth Street, then only four blocks later at Eighteenth Street before rolling into Twenty-third Street evokes a Jamesian past in the traveler's imagination of Manhattan. Every trip on that line recalls his descriptions in *Washington Square,* of a city aerated by fields and meadows below midtown and above the business district where ease—at least in the turns of James's sentences— prevailed. The layout of stations on the IRT suggests that it might be immoderate for travelers in the mold of the novel to be required to walk a distance that might exceed four street blocks.

We are no less prone to imagine the passage on the former IND line from Columbus Circle to 125th Street on the D or A trains as the space of a light-year. The time spent in the swoosh and clickety-clack of a train barreling north or south, through local stations (Seventy-second Street, Eighty-first Street, Ninety-sixth Street . . .) that flash by, marks in the daily life of a traveler going from midtown to 168th Street and beyond a limit-experience of human endurance, especially at rush hour in the dog days of July. If an art of travel were ever conceivable in New York, it might have been, before the city was laced with interstate highways and tied to Staten Island by the Verrazano Bridge (along with other automotive monuments were synchronized with the building of the World's Fair of 1964), the child's pilgrimage on the D train from Manhattan to the New Yorker's *finis terra,* Coney Island, a secular Santiago de Compostela washed by the tides lapping New York harbor. The hours and hours a child had to while away in eager expectation of rides on the Ferris wheel or the roller coaster (a compressed elevated, the ultimate model of rapid transit) made Coney Island a fairyland of cotton candy and sleaze at the end of the line.

The New Yorker visiting Paris quickly marvels at the history of urban design that elided private, local, and national interests with stunning success. Where else could be found the rock-solid historical fact of myriad *correspondances* located at strategic points where the lines crisscross over and again? No wonder that the principles of 1789 seem best illustrated in the metro. The dream of the engineer Fulgence Bienvenüe was to have a station no more than four hundred meters from any point in the city. His chart was a democracy conflating rail and republic. By contrast, the New York Metropolitan Transit Authority (MTA), because of the history of private investments and the rivalries of different enterprises, is efficient cause for civic and even national embarrassment. *Correspondances* in Manhattan are few and far between. The unilateral design leaves the metaphoric imagination impoverished. Of the three parallel north–south lines, the east and west sides of the IRT and the IND meet only at Fifty-ninth Street. Only at Broadway-Nassau and Fulton Street, near the antipodes of the island, do all three lines share an interchange. For inhabitants who know Paris, the "Forty-second Street Shuttle" between east and west IRT has always seemed an alibi or a weak concession to French innovation synchronous with the invention of the Statue of Liberty. To venture crossing, at the cost of one fare, from the Upper West Side to the eastern side of Manhattan, the traveler is obliged to take as many as four lines.

The New York trains are given to speed, whereas the metro seems charmingly (or exasperatingly, depending on the passenger's mood) deliberate in its passage from one station to the next. The slowness seems to tell travelers to "chill out and enjoy our city." In Manhattan, acceleration implies that outside of waiting for the next train, the passenger can be relieved of having to meditate on fate, time, alienation, or the subway itself. For the New Yorker, all time is constrained. In Paris, the contrary prevails (despite Henri Lefebvre's pronouncements on the subject). The subway happens to be a glycerine, added to thought, that slows ratiocination and allows thus for Cartesian clarity and distinctness to come to inchoate musings. The snail's pace seems designed to raise consciousness, not only on or about transport, but about the virtues as much of meditation as mediation. The station resembles the *poêle* in which Descartes slowly warmed to his discovery of the cogito. Where almost every subway in North America is equipped with sliding doors that open and close automatically, and that warn the child to stay clear of their operation, the metro builds into its system a means of rehearsing and celebrating a subjectivity where action ensues thinking. The *loqueteaux* or door handles that the traveler is obliged to flip backward or forward when entering or exiting the train require a minimal but decisive gesture, reminding everyone that he or she lives in an unflinchingly post-Sartrian world in which "being-for-oneself" is felt when we open the door by our own decision and means. An entire style or "way of doing" or practicing the subway begins with thinking about when and how to open the door. Similar reflection comes with the muffled bang of the folding seat or *strapontin* that hits the wall behind when a rider abandons the chair. Americans would probably associate this mechanism with French exceptionalism concerning economy (during rush hour) or consumption (in the "hollow" times) of space when they behold riders who abruptly decide to stand, in a gesture of metropolitan community, at the site where they had been sitting just seconds before.

Augé notes that the poetry of the metro seems to flow in the affect aroused by its names. Within the metropolitan circuit, where the subway was first traveled, the place-names conveyed the sense of a national history. As the traveler goes further outward, transgressing the former walls of the city at the time of the birth of the system (July 19, 1900), topographical names overtake those chosen to commemorate a certain past. "Perfectly exotic" names in the eyes of "traditional Parisians" sometimes recall "the ideas of barrier and departure," such as at "Saint-Denis-Porte de Paris" or "Aubervilliers-Pantin-Quatre Chemins." Certain uncanny motivations arise from the linkages of the most patriotic of all places, "Charles de Gaulle-Étoile," with the terminus of the line serving the station ending at "Nation." Étoile, a place-name that became the title of Patrick Modiano's *La Place de l'Étoile,* reflects the Franco-Jewish heritage of the postwar years by being confused with the yellow patch worn by victims of the Occupation. The toponym conjures up much of what Augé first recalled—the painful images, perpetuated in newsreels, of Nazi troops marching under the Arc de Triomphe in 1940.

Americans are hard put to meld language and place with such polyvocal innuendo. It takes a Texan tourist to commit a crime of lèse-majesté when he insists that Houston Street must be a row of tawdry townhouses when he is told he can't dipthongize the name as it ought to be pronounced, in the name of the founder of the Lone Star State, in the twang of "Hewston." New Yorkers face a difficult task when they motivate the numerical place-names of their stops. A resident of Manhattan might infuse Seventy-second Street with the odor of bagels and knishes bought from Zabar's at half price on Monday mornings. Forty-second Street and the Port Authority carry the memory of a Nedick's hot-dog stand that wafted the odor of rotten orange peels with burnt frankfurters in the atmosphere of the crossing of the Eighth Avenue lines and the entry to the bus terminal. Delancy, by contrast, is forever confused with delinquency around the odor of sauerkraut and french fries at Katz's delicatessen. Lexington Avenue on the IND is less a station than an endless escalator.

New York stops give over to memory with difficulty. They cannot rival with what inheres or is already given in the image of "Sèvres-Babylone"; the station of *La Traversée du Luxembourg* becomes one of the secrets of *In the Metro.* There the drama of subjectivity is heard in the severance and breakage of porcelain from Sèvres down the road and the isolation of a "baby alone," or a local barbarian's *babil-on* amid the debauchery of hanging gardens and nude bodies remembered from *Intolerance.* Or a stop such as "Cambronne" can only cause the rider to smile at the thought of the history of the subway and of sewage flowing through both the word and its originator. The stop celebrates a substantive more than the person whom it eternizes. *Le mot de Cambronne* is a classic euphemism that invokes not just the patriotic gore of the Napoleonic era, but, in most likelihood, metaphor and personification in a broad sense.[10] Modestly francophone travelers who ride in Montreal for the first time may be prone to a misprision that tests the enduring quality, like *Cambronne,* of the place-names of the metro. Upon hearing the name of the *correspondance* "Berri-UQUAM," agglutinated in Canadian French ("Berukam"), for this provincial traveler the station in the city becomes the Napoleonic inverse of Cambronne, that is, "Bir-Hakeim," a stop on the same line, a stop that heralds the glory years of the Corsican emperor in his Egyptian campaigns at the eve of the nineteenth century. But "Berri-UQUAM," a proper name and an acronym for the University of Quebec at Montreal, even when given a new inflection thanks to an aural mistake, underscores how the construction of an identity is made with the displacement of foreign places of a past recalled in children's histories that are mapped out along the lines of subway stops.

If there is any motivation of so many directions and flashes of historical memories in the New York network, it would also be found in what the French might see, as did Louis-Ferdinand Céline in *Journey to the End of the Night* when he rose from a galley to behold a vertical island of unabashed power. It still overwhelms pedestrians reading the names of Rockefeller Center, the grisly touristic site of the former World Trade Center, at Astor Place and, above all, Wall Street, the place where Herman Melville, long before Céline's Bardamu arrived in New York in a slave ship, erected a macadam barrier between language and world in his "Bartleby the Scrivener." It was then a city-fiction, a work about Manhattan that bore the legend of "A Wall-Street Story." Surely no place-name on Manhattan Island could rival the grace that rhymes with the rough but fond touch of Breton granite at "Filles du Calvaire." The reader of the toponym on line 8 of the metro is wont to wonder if penitent whores, displaced from the rue Saint-Denis, populate the landscape of an urban calvary. The only jocular parallel for a New Yorker would be found in the sight of the penultimate stop of the Broadway line at the apical tip of Manhattan (when looking north), where "Dyckman Street" is next to 207th Street on the IRT, at whose point a cryptic eros is graphed on the MTA map, where the abstract plan of the island begins to resemble a phallus, suggesting that the streets are littered with sex workers, and all the more since the site is served only occasionally, according to indications on the subway maps of New York, and mostly during "rush hours." But here the play is contrived, whereas in Paris, the place-names seem to come naturally.

II

It is difficult to believe that the history of the metro reveals a network preceding the names attached to it. The exact nature of the grid, a subject of intense debate among city planners throughout the second half of the nineteenth century, was first seen on plans whose station-dots awaited the printing of their toponyms. On the first Garnier tourist maps depicting the network, printed to coincide with the inauguration of the subway and the Universal Exposition of 1900, a web of deep red lines is placed over the white channels of new and old boulevards. A fleshlike pink defines the inner city, on which are set frontal views of the principal monuments in keen detail in black and white. Lines alternately blend into and emerge from the space.

In the first touristic maps a sense of order and circumspection prevails. What was then the recently constructed peripheral railway, the "chemin de fer de ceinture," draws a parergon between the inner city and the surround of polygonal walls. The latter are pierced at the various gateways to the city, beyond which a green ecumene offers greenery and illusions of verdure on all sides. The bird's-eye perspective of this part of the map draws the eye toward undulating hills, vegetation, and hamlets extending along the bends of the Seine until a green horizon meets a cerulean strip of sky. The broad swath of the red lines indicating the pattern of the subway is grandiose next to the filigree of the *grandes lignes* of the French railways that extend from the five principal stations to an infinity of the countryside beyond Courbevoie, Genevilliers, Saint-Ouen, Aubervilliers, Alfortville, Vitry, and Vanves, sites where the promise of pastoral bliss is met by the thin furrows radiating outward from the pink center. That in fact engineers had established a rail gauge for the metro narrower than that of the major railways—to avoid absorption or takeover by private enterprise involved in the construction—is emphasized in reverse, the subway circuit drawn in a majestic swath of red lines in contrast to the thin meander of the great railroads.[11]

Comparison of two versions of the Garnier map shows that, all of a sudden, from an abstract webbing is born on the same map in its next stage a metrocity of place-names. Onto a state of urban nature is built a culture of names, of kinship, along with social and historical genealogies. The two states of the early map bear out the vision, shared by the structural anthropologists of the lineage of Rousseau, of an immediate passage that jumps from nature to symbolic process. If an ethnographer in the line of Lévi-Strauss and Augé laughs at visitors' efforts to motivate place-names and to attach mythological importance to their sound and shape (at the end of "Memories" in *In the Metro*), the shift between the one map and the next suggests that nomination is sudden and total. Names emerge from the map in order not to interfere with the architecture of the monuments. The red color of the characters melds with the pink background, conferring the adjacent space with words that dissolve into the image. In both states the *Nouveau Paris Monumental* meticulously depicts edifices of every stripe (included is the flamboyant Saint-Séverin and a handsome profile of Saint-Médard at the foot of the rue Émile-Bernard (between the rue d'Ulm and the rue Monge, but without the rue Mouffetard in evidence). Now and again the lines cut through the buildings or monuments (the Chambre des Députés, the Tribunal de Commerce at the Cité, the sarcophagus of the Lion de Belfort at Denfert-Rochereau, etc.) or they skirt by others (the Arc de Triomphe, the Trocadéro Palace). The map is so carefully drawn that the dashed parallel lines that indicate the course of construction (in the line from Cambronne to Opéra) are covered with a solid trace of red ink, designating rapid progess in construction. In the map in its first state, the lines are in place but carry much less ink: the line from Porte d'Auteuil to Opéra is marked under construction, as is the circuit from Opéra to Place des Fêtes. The later version shows that much more work is completed in the space of a short duration of time.

And comparison of the Garnier map with a plan depicting the current state of the Paris metro in 1911, printed and dated

April of that year (at a scale of 1:25,000), shows that suddenly the metro line has gained autonomy over the city.[12] The network is applied to the map, the dots representing stations that are monuments of abstraction that seem to confirm the victory of the "flatbed" style over the illusion of depth that had marked the buildings and landscapes of the work of 1901. Now the map is a diagram of quasi-circular and axial configurations. The *cardo* (north–south) and *decumanus* (east–west) lines, taken from Roman planning, construe Paris to be the center of the circle defined by the north and south components of line 2 bisecting line 1.[13] The orthogonals extending from Porte de Choisy and Place d'Italie to Invalides, from Porte de Picpus (now Porte Dorée) to Louvre, from Porte de Montreuil to République, and from Pelleport to Porte des Lilas are all set in place. The map shows that a good deal of the inner circuit of Paris, between the north–south axis (Porte de Clignancourt/Porte d'Orléans; Porte de la Villette/Place d'Italie), and within the circle about Paris (at that time Nation-Italie-Denfert-Grenelle-Étoile-Villiers-Villette-Rue d'Allemagne) remains to be completed, but that the future is almost past, and what would become the geographic character of the twentieth-century metro is already a fact. The accelerated speed with which a new system of transport is engineered, named, and connected figures in the rhetoric of the map of 1911 all the while the design reveals how much it is informed by a complex historical backdrop.

The subway operated within a deeply embedded history of omnibus and carriage lines that furrowed the city practically from the time it was called Lutèce. Most literary historians would begin reflections on the metro with Montaigne's "Des coches" (Of coaches), an ethnographic meditation on metaphors and modes of transport in which the essayist compares the effect of palanquins, both land and water coaches, ships, and pedestrian travel on political subjects. In the dense composition of the essay the reader catches glimpses of everyday life in sixteenth-century Paris. The Louvre is a work site; the Pont-Neuf, in scaffolding, will not be completed before the end of the writer's life; the outer walls are being redesigned in view of new modes of warfare. The city that the author loved "jusques à ses verrues et ses tasches" (right down to its warts and blemishes) bustles with many a wagon and litter. Montaigne shows that when it rolled through the city a golden coach was, like today's Range Rover, a symbol of luxury exacerbating social contradiction.

When, in the seventeenth century, the population expanded at the rate of geometrical progression, the streets became clogged with rented carriages. Called *fiacres,* they owed their name to a statue of a patron saint in the courtyard of a building at the corner of the rue Saint-Martin and the rue de Montmorency. There Nicolas Sauvage began in 1630 a new and lucrative enterprise.[14] Carriages such as the *fiacre* were hailed in the streets or others, *sous remise,* were leased from stables. Royal patents served as drivers' and chauffeurs' licenses. Omnibus coaches went regularly (but not on designated schedules) from Paris to Versailles and from the city through Le Pecq to Saint-Germain and back again. *Calèches* were open-air four-wheelers that carried two couples behind a horse; *cabriolets* were their covered counterparts; *brouettes* were wheelbarrow-like two-wheelers pulled by one or several hacks. The litter was ubiquitous. *Coches d'eau* bore travelers from the shores of the Seine to the outskirts along the bends and buckles of the river. For a short time (1662–77) eight-seater omnibuses circulated within Paris. Only in 1828 did these larger vehicles return to the streets, at the beginning of the "golden age" of horse-drawn wagons, of which were counted 2,542 rental vehicles in 1819. In 1853, the number "rose brutally to 5,442," a figure that included 1,992 *fiacres* and 3,450 rented carriages. The return of the omnibus promised a rational system of itineraries, as parking regulations, in response to the increasing flow of traffic, were soon decreed by the city's prefect of police in cooperation with the EGO (Entreprise générale des omnibus). In 1853, a larger vehicle, the *Impériale,* was designed to carry more than twenty passengers. The construction of the *Petite ceinture* railway, begun in 1852, was completed in 1869.

By the time the demography of Paris swelled from 546,856 in 1801 to 1,053,261 in 1851, urban planners felt that railways could be prolongated into and either above or below the city. The influx of tourists in the Second Empire, thanks to the progress of rail travel, manufacture, and tourism, grew critically at the time of the Imperial Exposition where, in 1855, the city welcomed twenty-five million visitors. In 1870, the sight of the "tramway hippomobile," a horse-drawn trolley, made manifest the idea of an electric railway. Soon the CGO (Compagnie générale des omnibus) would consider different designs and blueprints for innovation. The debates and decisions that ensued paved the way for the future subway.

The idea of a metropolitan railway had been spawned as early as 1840. If we were to correlate the history of Parisian transports with Baudelaire's "Correspondances," a sonnet arguably of the same vintage, it might be concluded that the author was—however much he would have despised the fact—a leader and a visionary of urban planning.[15] A cornerstone in the architecture of *Les Fleurs du Mal*, the poem maps out a synesthesia of travel in which metaphysical and real itineraries crisscross and diverge. Anticipating later verse that tells of inhumanly compressed urban times and spaces, "Correspondances" may be one of the great subway poems of French literature. The lyric has fascinated anthropologists for its way of correlating fugacious movement of sensation with translation.

> La Nature est un temple où de vivants piliers
> Laissent parfois sortir de confuses paroles
>
> [Nature is a temple in which living pillars
> Sometimes let confused speech be heard]

This first line of the poem compares a structure, such as that of the Madeleine of Paris, to a woodland. Claude Lévi-Strauss compared the *vivants piliers,* generally understood to be trees, to the totem poles he beheld in the American Museum of Natural History in New York (which he no doubt accessed by the

Eighty-first Street stop on the IND local) during the Occupation.[16] There might have lingered in his mind the contrastive image of black, rivet-studded I-beams in the station just below the museum.

The presence of the subway implied in both the title of the poem and in Lévi-Strauss's cursory reading might inspire analysis that brings together the labors of anthropology and history. First, city planners of the nineteenth century indeed conceived an urban "nature" to be a network of lines and "temples" from which a new and rich panoply of sensation and social activity would emerge. Would not the train that eager travelers on the platform seek to hear entering the station come both from *within* their expectations and from *without,* from the tunnel they stare into in hope of seeing light approaching from the end, "Comme de longs échos qui de loin se confondent" (Like long echos that from afar are mixed)? If an automated railroad is anticipated fifty years *before* its realization, Baudelaire's "Nature" could refer to a future subway stop, such as "Nation," or else the entire urban system of rails that grids the urban experience he describes in his *Petits poèmes en prose.* The city would be post-Nature itself. As a metonym, the "stop" or hemistich in his Alexandrines would be at once, like all future stations in the metro, a metaphor and a synecdoche of Paris at the center of its own line of description. Those "forests of symbols" would be tantamount to the sudden growth of station names defining the population's kinship through a logic affixing names to places.

And, as Augé strives to show in his work on the poetry of the metro, the *correspondance,* the title of the poem, would be the sign par excellence of what it means to live both in Paris and in society at large: individuals sense best their plight and pleasure qua individuals in the subway, but they also discover how they are determined, tracked, located, or even born and mapped into configurations beyond their grasp. That subway travelers "can always change lines and stations" (he notes in the last sentence of the book) for lack of escaping the network, or that they can take "some beautiful detours," attests to the exhilarating and crushing truths obtained when Baudelaire's poem is super-imposed on the historical map of the metro.

Baudelaire was also precocious when he anticipated the advent of the subway through aroma. The sonnet "turns"—literally, it corresponds with itself, it shifts its own registers or directions—in "line 8" (comparable to Balard-Creteil?) where "Les parfums, les couleurs et les sons se répondent" (Perfumes, colors, and sounds answer each other). Baudelaire transforms intellect into sensation, *savoir* into *saveur,* through confusion of grammatical direction (cardinal movement, or *sens*) and feeling *(sens),* when "line 14" (the last and ultimate of the metro, the "Météor" from Madeleine to Tolbiac?) tells of odors "Qui chantent les transports de l'esprit et des sens" (That sing of the transports of the mind and sensation).[17] Among the perfumes enumerated are those of children's flesh, amber, musk, benjamin (anticipating the name of his future translator and apologist?), and, of course, incense. In *In the Metro* Augé tends not to bring forward the aromas of the metro, but he does equate the Baudelairean *correspondance* with the theme of his book both in the title of the last section and in his descriptions of the many persons who "change" stations as they might move from one discipline or practice to another.

If a passage from Baudelaire to Augé can be imagined,[18] the poet's nose is transformed into the anthropologist's intuition. It is perhaps because, implies Augé, the amplitude of the practice of urban anthropology needs to include some of the relation of odors to lineage and social spaces and their attendant contradictions. Baudelaire showed that aroma is a basis for the cultivation of perception and sensation. "Thick" historians of Paris have combined archival work with a search for the sensation of everyday life in past epochs. Michel de Certeau long ago argued for histories treating of the objects people handled, local speech, ways of ambulating from a barn to a kitchen, the fashion of digging furrows along hedgerows, or how tools are raised in the air in the excitement of peasants' revolts.[19] Alain Corbin has painted vivid pictures of the relation of odor, space, and bodily practice in the French city. Others have alighted on the public *urinoir* and treatment of refuse and litter to show where demarcations between places dangerous and appealing are drawn, and how everyday life is organized and negotiated by divisions, as Mary Douglas has shown in a pragmatic way, between spaces pure and dangerous or seductive and repulsive. The Parisian metro is thus the apple of the social historian's eye. It would not be presumptuous to affirm that Baudelaire, after Sébastien Mercier and before Proust and Lévi-Strauss, counts among the finest chroniclers of the odors of a city developing its underground dimensions in the mix of other smells, "rich and triumphant," "bearing the expansion of infinite things" (lines 11 and 12) of "Correspondances."

The voice of "Élévation," the poem immediately preceding "Correspondances," asks its mind (the poem is in dialogue with its *esprit*), to carry it "loin de ces miasmes morbides" (far from these morbid miasmas). The subway rider of the R.E.R., say, en route from the sanitized station of Roissy-Aéroport Charles de Gaulle to the center of the city, who rolls into the lower depths of the Châtelet *correspondance* from the Gare du Nord, often feels prone to faint in the fumes of hydrogen sulfide emanating from adjacent sewage. The odors make Châtelet, the name of a fortress demolished in 1802, once the seat of the criminal jurisdiction of Paris, smell of things foul. Tourists and dwellers alike avoid changing trains at the station known for both olfactory and human malevolence. If that stop is an emblem of Baudelaire's morbid miasmas, his injunction, "Va te purifier dans l'air supérieur" (go and purify yourself in the upper atmosphere) could be construed to mean that subway riders at Châtelet ought to get above ground or find an elevated line (such as number 6) that will refresh the lungs.

Here and elsewhere the verse of *Les Fleurs du Mal* encapsulates past history of Parisian archaeology and anticipates future speleology of the subway. Many of the debates surrounding the creation of the metro in fact hinged on the election to elevate—(as in "Élévation") or to excavate (as in "Spleen" [lxxv]), where

"L'âme d'un vieux poète erre dans la gouttière' [line 7] [the soul of an old poet wanders in the gutter]). Simultaneously, the success of the London West End "tube" in 1863 inspired French engineers to dig underground, but only after they had entertained numerous plans for elevated trains connecting the major monuments, or even steam-driven locomotives pulling wagons up and down the Seine on rails erected over the middle of the river.[20] The double postulation was such that one of the schemes "included a system of tunnels to be used for passenger trains by day and as sewers by night" in which specially designed ventilators would clear the air every morning.[21] A double bind was erected: what would be visually odious above could only be countered by a something putridly odorous below. It may be that aroma and the rhythm of diurnal and nocturnal character was literally written into the system on the grounds that a metro was urgently needed to circulate foods to the Halles by way of an underground railway, or that the subway might serve to actualize some utopian schemes, such as what Victor Hugo concocted in *Les Misérables*, in which conduits carrying human excrement would be pumped out of the bowels of Paris to flow in the furrows of beet fields to the north and west, the fruits of which would be transported by rail back to the core of the city to feed an ever-hungry public. The railroad, for a long time an emblem of pollution, was soon to be cleansed with the subway, a train driven by electricity.

Complicating these casual impressions of history is what we can make of Haussmann's ethnic cleansing. Standard historical tracts tell us that he cut swaths of boulevards into the city in order, first, to divide and conquer so that different areas would be demarcated by wide avenues and, second, that their breadth would allow the forces of the Second Empire quick deployment of armed police in order to quell strife of the kind remembered from 1830 and 1848. Hindsight might reveal another motive. With the wide avenues, subways could be dug far more economically than by having them tunneled under extant buildings. The urban repression and creation of new space that led to boredom (as Flaubert notes in *Bouvard et Pécuchet* and Henry James in "Occasional Paris," a tourist's article published in 1884) or agoraphobia in fact gave rise to democratic transport that has since become the urban *mode d'emploi* to lessen pollution and discourage automotive transport.

We begin to see that in matters of odor the history and anthropology of the subway are intimately related. The debates of the 1880s summed up the fears and delights already cast into Baudelaire's Alexandrines twenty or thirty years earlier. And the unique aromas of the metro forever exude in its toponyms. If what Montaigne, in the gleeful pessimism of his epic inversion of the medieval world picture (the "Apologie de Raimond Sebond") called the "dungheap of the world" is found at Châtelet or in the spirit of Cambronne, its stench is surely sanitized at "Javel," where the word ("Eau de Javel," the French name for Clorox) brings forward the acrid odor of chlorine and sulfur doused over rot. Gobelins, the site that Rabelais celebrated with a toponymic tale of canine urination to explain why a smell of ammonia surrounds the Bièvre River, surely has its counterpart at Saint-Sulpice.[22] Saint-Ambroise and the Porte des Lilas offer perfumes to counter the stink imagined in these names and inhaled in many corridors of *correspondances.* One of the marvelous conundrums in the history of odor and redeployment of the subway—of an ingenuity that knows how to *faire avec,* to do something practical but *other* with given inventions—concerned its viability as a refuge of civil defense in the 1930s. Signs of the diastrous effects of mustard gas in the trenches of 1914–18 were still immediate. The subway was to provide hermetic havens of clean air in the event that Germany relaunched a chemical offensive. Stations below six meters underground were chosen to house sealed panels that would insulate the platforms from the air above in the event of gas attacks.[23]

But for the everyday ethnologist who follows his or her nose, the metro offers an incomparable olfactory range. At the Place Monge, near where Augé lived, on Sunday morning shoppers bring the aromas of cheese and freshly butchered meat or charcuterie into the station. Often the Place des Fêtes is inflected with cumin, garlic, and exotic spices that waft from bodies pressed together during rush hour. A clammy and stale delight, mixed with a bouquet of muscadet, greets some travelers at the Gare Saint-Lazare by an entry giving onto a café that shucks and sells all sizes of oysters. Everywhere the trains and stations mix the effects of sweat permeating clothing with the butts of Gauloises and Gitanes. Poetasters in the line of Duchamp are likely to think that the metro, born under the enigma of the R.A.T.P. ("What does it stand for?") carries the sign of sewers in the *rat* of its name, or else the flunky aspect (noted when riders are frustrated and annoyed) of an operation destined to *rater*.[24] Odors in the subway inspire others to gloss the Duchampian acronym as a way of "circulating your flatulence and getting away with it" (*Ars petandi in honeste societate,* a title that Rabelais imagined in the Librairie Saint-Victor on the Left Bank in *Pantagruel*)—air (R) à (A) tes (T) pets (P)—in the collective press of bodies, in consonance with what Céline noted during the Depression in his *Journey to the End of the Night,* apropos of the world below Wall Street, in "le communisme joyeux du caca" (the joyous communism of turd).

In a foreseeable future of the metro, aroma may be a matter of mind. The newest and greatest of all tourist attractions in Paris is the *ligne 14,* the subway linking Madeleine on the right bank to Tolbiac where, across the river, the four towers from the new Bibliothèque de France rise ominously into the sky. The subway is composed of cars linked to each other by pliable, accordion-like walls that squeeze or extend when the train follows the curves and bends of the track. Without any real partition between each car, the train offers a perspective that runs along the entire horizontal axis of its interior; when the train rolls on a straight stretch of track, the rider can catch a view of the inside of the whole train. Passengers can run to the front to watch the stations approaching. They can circulate rapidly, with less fear of panhandlers or beggars, who are given equal right to sweep through the train without having to open doors or exit and reenter at each stop.

Most of all, the rider can marvel at its *driverless mechanism*, the ultimate solution to the Cartesian machinery of a soul or a driver in the cockpit of a bodily wagon or nacelle. The new train, the Météore, would be the metro etherealized, a utopian dream of the mechanical bent of French ingenuity.[25] Since its inauguration in October 1998, the aroma is of plexiglass, and space-age polystyrene. Human odors accrete with difficulty in the microscopic pores of plastic, but over time they may bring a refreshing uncanniness that mixes the sanitized air of a computer store with odors of sweaty bodies. And why not: for the train begins at Madeleine, the dirty and squat church miming a Greek temple and recalling "Correspondances" that is the homonym of the spongy pastry whose odor and texture, when soaked with tea, inaugurates Proust's voyage in search of lost time. That the train soon ends near a comparatively grandiose edifice suggests that the R.A.T.P. subscribes to Mitterrand's legacy of monumentality. But a poetic fact of the metro remains: a Proustian terminus is served by an archive equipped to analyze the work and to protect oblivion from further decay. The seemingly odorless and robotic line seems to be built on the olfactory memory of the other subway lines that can be found in the bowels of the Bibliothèque de France. The new line is inhabited by a new and different erotic presence. The recorded voice of a woman seductively announces the names of each approaching station. In the classical subway, the gaze cast upon bodies of proximate riders (with fantasies of the kind celebrated in Cobean's cartoons of the *New Yorker* of years past), the fantasy of meeting a desired other or of retrieving moments of fleeting attraction (which Augé delights in recounting both in *La Traversée du Luxembourg* and toward the end of "Solitudes"), is written into the grain of her speech. When the train whirs toward Châtelet, she whispers mellifluously, "SHA-tuh-lay," the tonic accent falling on the first syllable, as if the name were a body available and free for the pleasure of every passenger.

Reflecting on his Parisian adolescence, in *Les mots* Jean-Paul Sartre implies that the absurdity of human life on planet Earth began in the system of control and conduct in subways and railroads. He discovered that he was of no use and had no raison d'être when, riding in public transport, he found himself bereft of a ticket. Without his stub he would fail to comply with the social contract of the underground; he would be in violation for lack of an identity tag. Sartre's *prise de conscience* causes foreigners to smile. In other systems a token or a plastic card allows access to the illusion of freedom to circulate and to escape the system alive and well, whereas in Paris the specter of the law, of a controlling agent, the inspector, the gatekeeper at the end of the line, the Saint Peter of the Metro, haunts every rider. At the end of a day or two, the traveler empties pockets so cluttered with canceled tickets (a menace of the washing machine) that he or she wonders why there remains a need for a closure for which the ticket is the Parisian's viaticum and sign of salvation. Does the system exist to force recall of the time when squat and plump women, the *poinçonneuses* seated at the entry to the platforms, punched the tickets so that a social exchange would be assured? So that the beginning of a Maussian relation of obligation to the R.A.T.P. and the human community in general would ensure the rider's socialization by virtue of forcing utterance of a *bonjour* or a *merci* en route to the train? Or else, at the exit, in our time where no one stands to gather the spent stubs, does the automatic gate (or *portillon*) of the R.E.R., opened when the paper is slipped into and sucked through its slot, remind the rider that in the age of automatism all humans, travelers and ticket takers alike, are more superfluous than Sartre had ever imagined?

These questions can be approached, like the automatic turnstile, from different angles. At the end of *Tristes Tropiques* Lévi-Strauss remarked that the universe began without humans and would, in the greater scheme of things, outlive them. The exit machine surely reminds the rider of the fortuitous character of passage in the world in which the subway will survive humanity.

Augé intuits the point toward the end of his essay by noting that
at every minute of its operation the metro carries riders who are
taking their first trips while others are taking their last. The subway surely exceeds the ends of humanity. But Augé's remark
cannot be seen outside of his concept of the *nonplace,* developed
in *Non-lieux,* in which he shows how much the modern world
constructs innocuous and disconcerting or tepidly enervating
areas for which privilege is required in order to enter. Such are
the waiting rooms in airports, accessible only to designated per-
sonnel (bearing photographic images of themselves in laminat-
ed plastic cards clipped to their chests) or travelers (equipped
with boarding passes), who pass by the avatar of the *poinçon-
neuse,* a third- or fourth-world baggage inspector who stares
listlessly at a television monitor hooked to a conveyer belt, or a
bouncer just beyond who brandishes a metal detector. Ditto for
the space for cars owned, leased, and rented; the admission to a
bank or a haberdashery in an urban area that is electronically
surveiled; or bookstores and libraries with electronic controls.
In the broader scope of Augé's writing, the ticket to the metro is
a first sign, albeit an already degraded one, of entry into a nonplace, with the adumbrated exception that the democracy of the
subway, part and parcel of its history, attenuates the sense of
privilege. Almost anyone can get into the metro, but its space is
not so vapidly consumerist as an authentic *non-lieu.*[26] Everyone
can get out, but sometimes the ticketless riders, either by ruse or
by need, as the Beatles used to sing, seek "a little help from their
friends" at the turnstile, who hold open the door or pass a ticket
back to the troubled soul who can't escape the *huis-clos* of the
exit gate. The action affirms once again that a community exists,
and that Mauss's conclusions about obligation are countered by
the *acte gratuit* of tiny events of generosity. The ticket assures
entry into a network bearing comparison to the nonplace.[27]

Yet the ticket carries a metaphysical dimension that neither
Sartre nor Augé has addressed. An axiom of deixis might state
that any "shifter" designates at once where a subject is and
where he or she is not. The many jokes about puzzled tourists

staring at the maps on signboards outside a subway station, alternately staring at their copies of the *Paris par arrondissement* pocket guide, the environing landscape, and the arrow on the map adjacent to the words stating "Vous êtes ici" always affirm that we are never where we are said to be.[28] The ticket seems to assuage the disquiet of displacement wrought by the skewed relation of the map to the territory. It assures not just a reason for traveling, but also, quasi-unconsciously, it bears a map that would guide the Baudelairean traveler within the subway to the dream of a destination "anywhere out of this world." The rhetoric of the ticket is crafted to suscitate the reverie.

Comparisons show why. A New Yorker, putting a token in the palm of the hand, discovers a rich and unsettling iconography. Seen over the lifelines of the hand, the striations radiating from a central void of a pentagon cut punched out of the alloy inspire fear about the meaning of a five-sided stigma, a black hole that seems to remain on the hand, each edge of the design symbolizing one of the five boroughs within reach of the coin's bearer. The thicker and heavier token admitting its user to the Boston subway prints on its reverse a great T within a circle recalling the great T/O maps of antiquity and the Middle Ages. These memory-icons offered schemata of the known world by devising a partition of continents by which a capital T was drawn inside of a containing circle. The outer edge was the ecumene signaled by a great "ocean-sea." Inside, the T is drawn to put in the lower left area Europe (bequeathed by Noah to Jaseth), to the right Africa (given to Cham), and the great area above, Asia (inherited by Sem). The coin displays an *orbis terrarum* that divides the world into the three known continents by virtue of the trumeau of the letter designating the Mediterranean and the lintel the juncture of the Red Sea and the Tanaïs or Danube Rivers. The ecumene of the *mare oceanum* in which are printed the letters of the Metropolitan Boston Transit Authority signals that the design of the world at large is within reach of the traveler's fingers, or that he or she might wish to take the train to the continents borne by the coin.

The current metro ticket bears a fluvial emblem, the line of the Seine tracing the profile of, perhaps, a comely female whose chin, mouth, nose, and eyeline cut through the ecumene as might a river goddess, a variant of Villon's Flora of the great ballad "Les femmes du temps jadis," whose waters flow from antiquity through Paris and out to Normany and Rouen, where the most fabled of all French maidens, Joan of Arc, was sacrificed in the hope of a perpetual return of fluids cleansing and enriching French lands and cities. The woman seems to whisper a praise of nature that would otherwise be forgotten in the urban depths of Paris. Next to her profile are the circles that enclose the signs of the metro, the bus, the inner-city R.E.R. and the T/O *mappa mundi*. Where the New York token signals the confinement of the network, and the Boston coin an aide-mémoire of an ancient world bequeathed to the sons of Noah and the invitation to go seaward, the Parisian ticket obeys a gently seductive calling, a whispered invitation, to swim in a suspended state of voyage. The waters of the city are recalled with an erotic pull not evident in the motto of Paris, *fluctuat nec mergitur,* printed under the emblem of a ship floating on wavy waters under a sky of fleurs-de-lis.

The rider beholding the ticket is susceptible to Leibnizian fantasy about spaces outside, of an infinity beyond, while remaining on the opaque inner surface of a map and the urban totality. The ticket holder in the train would be in something resembling a medium-sized monad between the traveler's biological body and the sensation of the infinite cosmos. The ticket would offer signs of romantic elevation all the while beckoning worlds beyond the confines of the metropolitan circuit. The printed sign on the turquoise card recalls the appeal of the logo of the first northern buckle of the metro (currently line 2) on which the ecliptic band of a globe assumed the shape of a train rolling "around the world." Both the logo and the ticket assure the user of an illusion to move beyond, not-here, in the oceanic totality of the world at large, while riding along the periphery of the circuit. Something of a post-Baudelairean "invitation au voyage" is carried in a symbolism that the Surrealists of Paris took quite literally. Akin to automatic writing, they developed a practice of "voyages of cretinization" by which they put themselves in a state of suspension before descending into the metro and letting their feet lead them to any number of *correspondances*.[29]

By way of a circular conclusion, we can affirm that when images of the city of Paris, its metro (including the R.E.R., the R.A.T.P., and the suburban trains), its maps of streets, bus lines, and subways, its signs and objects that are the token elements of its everyday life are so mixed in the flux of the passenger's thoughts, they seem to bespeak the Borgesian axiom stating that "the map is not the territory." Surely the impact of the globe and its continents on a ticket or a coin offers a scale inverse to the dream expressed in Borges's story "On Rigor in Science," in which a map of a nation, planned on a 1:1 scale, covered the lands it represented. But for the ethnologist in the Parisian subway, the persisting memory of the map of colored lines drawn along and over the major thoroughfares is forever confused with the fragmentary impressions of specific streets, sites, or reflections. Augé's blur of a German soldier wearing a grey cap who was crossing the Place Maubert melds into a one-to-one relation with metaphor or transport. The student of the metro, its sufficient user and participant in its history and practice, rarely reaches the ecstasy of a subway sublime. The condition would be the underground equivalent of a mystical voyage. But he or she can always make a collage of a mental map with shards of life at large, always mediating the unacknowledged truth of the map with fortuitous passage in subterranean tunnels and, time permitting, rides on lines of limited choice. The subway map, when its projection is shot through the experience of the rider, invites speculation on one-to-one equivalence of life and urban space. We might say that the cartography of affect, which is one of the real contributions of Augé's works in the arena of everyday life, will have as a limit point the mystical sensation of the passenger's body—our body—being in measure of the world.

This fantasy may indeed be one of the many secrets running through *In the Metro*. The anthropologist who returns from the Alladian Lagoon to study the metro affronts the indomitable task of looking at a network endowed with a rich and debated history. Traditionally, the anthropologist takes as a point of departure the study of cultures without written chronicle. Augé discovered in Africa that anthropology could not live without colonial history. In his work he reveals that his brand of urban ethnology requires that the past be flattened or spatialized into a legible picture so that the *ideo-logic* of the circuit, the city, and its mixed demographies can find recognizable shape and contour. If a history intervenes, it comes through the private and collective worlds of life, led in different subways, that reflect on custom and happiness. The reader of his tract discovers that the affective relations with the metro and other modes of public transport extend the net of inquiry over a multinational area, over metrocities of different styles, histories, and speeds of evolution.

In the line of *In the Metro,* from station chapters leading from memories to solitudes, and from solitudes to correspondences before arriving at conclusions, we witness a plot that mixes any of the fourteen (or then, at the time of the writing of the book, thirteen) *lignes* with the itineraries of a narrative not unlike what is given in *La Traversée du Luxembourg.* From a disruption, the recall of an unsettling past (the German soldier at the Place Maubert in 1940), begins a voyage that objectifies reminiscence into literature before an encounter with solitude prompts resolution by affording the idea of a practice of imaginary and social travel. Even if it is within a controlling network, through ruse, choice, and metaphor, an invention—or, better, a creative intervention—results. The fellow rider, the reader of *In the Metro,* finds that perhaps the solitude wrought by news of the disappearance of a cherished friend (recounted in the first paragraph of the second chapter) has its own remedy, its mark as a Maussian gift of obligation, in the collective quality of the subway ride. Suddenly the self erodes and dissolves into an anonymity defined by the press and sensation of transit, in spaces that, at least on certain occasions, are not wholly co-opted or controlled. We are all in the train, but we are riding along different routes. It may be that the author of *La Traversée du Luxembourg,* who discovered at the end of his day of reflection that disquiet was vital to his happiness, made the mistake of going to the airport in a taxi. Had the R.E.R. been available, he would have taken the metro.

Notes

Introduction

I would like to thank Richard Morrison and Douglas Armato of the University of Minnesota Press; they have sustained this project and offered critical insights. Sections of the afterword were read in the context of the "Franz Boas" seminar in the Department of Anthropology at Columbia University in the winter of 2000. I would like to express gratitude to Ros Morris, Nick Dirks, Michael Taussig, and Janaki Bakhle for their encouragement and criticism. Bruno Bosteels has offered helpful commentary. David Cobb and Joe Garver of the Map Library at Harvard University have helped sort through cartographies of Paris over the past two centuries. David Thorstad has patiently read and corrected the translation. Anna Lakovitch has helped guide the project to completion. All errors are borne on my shoulders.

1. Two works in English can serve as starters. James Boon's *From Symbolism to Structuralism* (New York: Oxford University Press, 1972) is still a crucial treatment of the literary origins of the writings of Lévi-Strauss. He finds in Baudelaire and Mallarmé a poetics that motivates the ethnographer's personal and professional writings. Clifford Geertz's *Writers and Lives* (Princeton, N.J.: Princeton University Press, 1992) treats of the creative undercurrents of works ranging from Malinowski to Lévi-Strauss. Augé would merit a place in this field of speculation.

2. Augé's research on tourism is refracted in much of *In the Metro.* Tourism and investigation are the topic of *L'Impossible voyage: Le Tourisme et ses images* (Paris: Rivages, 1997).

3. To date, fifty-four titles have emerged from searches led in American and French libraries. He has written on painting and architecture and has even studied medieval travel literature. Some telling analyses of the reporting of the death of Princess Diana in French dailies are taken up in *Diana crash* (Paris: Descartes, 1998). His most recent work, of literary stamp, is *Fictions fin de siècle* (Paris: Fayard, 2000).

4. Marc Augé, *A Sense of the Other: The Timeliness and Relevance of Anthropology,* trans. Amy Jacobs (Stanford, Calif.: Stanford University Press, 1998), 3.

5. Derrida's critique was first published in a number of *Cahiers de la philosophie* on the topic "Lévi-Strauss in the Eighteenth Century" and then slightly revised and reprinted in *De la grammatologie* (Paris: Minuit, 1967).

6. Marc Augé, *Le Rivage alladian: Organisation et évolution des villages alladian* (Paris: Office de la Recherche Scientifique et Technique d'Outre-Mer [OSTROM], 1969).

7. Marc Augé, *Théorie des pouvoirs et idéologie: Étude de cas en Côte d'Ivoire* (Paris: Hermann, 1975).

8. "Events" are taken in the sense of Michel de Certeau's essay on May 1968 in chapters 1 and 2 of *The Capture of Speech*

and Other Political Writings, trans. Tom Conley (Minneapolis: University of Minnesota Press, 1997).

9. The definition comes and goes throughout *Théorie des pouvoirs et idéologie.* It is offered in concentrated form in Augé's introduction to a collection of essays titled *La Construction du monde: Religion, représentations, idéologie* (Paris: Maspero, 1974), 5–19, especially 17.

10. Augé, *Théorie des pouvoirs et idéologie,* 279. Through "wild ass's skin" Augé refers to Balzac's novel *La Peau de chagrin,* which tells of an ever-shrinking map of fate that the protagonist Raphaël de Valentin obtains in a Faustian bargain to defer his own suicide, a death indirectly caused by the impact of capital development in France at the time of the July Monarchy of 1830.

11. Jean Comaroff and John Comaroff, *Of Revelation and Revolution: Christianity, Colonialism, and Consciousness in South Africa* (Chicago and London: University of Chicago Press, 1991), 15. The Comaroffs' remarks are worth comparing to some of Georges Balandier's hypotheses that Augé mobilizes in *Théorie des pouvoirs et idéologie.* In *L'Anthropologie politique,* Balandier studies the exploitation of "traditionalisms" to the degree that they are imposed on indigenous peoples, and "pseudotraditionalisms" at the time of colonial change. A succession of "old" and "new" regimes is naturalized, and thus, as Augé summarizes, "the new political structure can be affirmed only in allowing itself to be translated in the former language" (*Théorie des pouvoirs et idéologie,* 304).

12. Augé appeals to Deleuze's introduction to Guattari's *Psychanalyse et transversalité* (Paris: Maspero, 1972), 414–15, in *Théorie des pouvoirs et idéologie.* It should be noted that the affiliation with Maspero indicates a politics of the left. Maspero, a publisher extinguished in the aftermath of 1968, had carried titles that addressed colonial ideology in general.

13. Marc Augé, *La Guerre des rêves: Exercices d'ethno-fiction* (Paris: Seuil, 1997), 146.

14. Deleuze's keenest pages on the *lieu quelconque* are devoted to the eradication of recognizable places in early postwar

cinema, at the end of *Cinéma 1: L'image-mouvement* (Paris: Minuit, 1983), 280–88, especially apropos of Rossellini's *Paisan.*

15. Marc Augé, *Non-lieux: Introduction à une anthropologie de la surmodernité* (Paris: Seuil, 1992), 58.

16. Marc Augé, (Paris: Payot, 1998).

17. Marc Augé, (Paris, Seuil, 1989).

18. Marc Augé, *Paris années trente: Roger-Viollet* (Paris: Hazan, 1996).

19. Marc Augé, (Paris: Hachette, 1985).

Memories

1. Claude Lévi-Strauss, *Race et histoire* (Paris: Gonthier, 1961).

2. Quoted in *Jours de France* 1568 (January 19–25, 1985).

3. Émile Durkheim, *Les Formes élémentaires de la vie religieuse,* 4th ed., (Paris: Presses Universitaires de France, 1979), 610.

Solitudes

1. Georges Perec, *Penser/Classer* (Paris: Hachette, 1985), 127–28.

2. Marcel Mauss, *The Gift: Forms and Functions of Exchange in Archaic Societies,* trans. Ian Cunnison (New York: Norton, 1967), 78.

3. Ibid.

4. Georges Gurvitch, "Avertissement de la première édition (1950)," to Marcel Mauss, *Sociologie et anthropologie,* précédé d'une Introduction à l'œuvre de Marcel Mauss par Claude Lévi-Strauss (Paris: Presses Universitaires de France, 1973), viii.

5. Mauss, *The Gift,* 77–78.

6. Claude Lévi-Strauss, *Introduction to the Work of Marcel Mauss,* trans. Felicity Baker (London: Routledge and Kegan Paul, 1987), 30–31.

7. Ibid., 33.

8. Ibid., 35.

9. Ibid., 37–38.

10. Mauss, *The Gift*, 76.

11. Ibid., 15.

Correspondences

1. Claude Lévi-Strauss, *Introduction to the Work of Marcel Mauss*, trans. Felicity Baker (London: Routledge and Kegan Paul, 1987), 16.

2. Ibid., 18.

3. Ibid., 19.

Afterword

1. Marc Augé, *La Traversée du Luxembourg: Ethno-roman d'une journée française considérée sous l'angle des mœurs de la théorie et du bonheur* (Paris: Hachette, 1985), 11.

2. Marc Augé, *Domaines et châteaux* (Paris: Seuil, 1989), 98–99.

3. Marcel Proust, "Nom de pays: Le nom," in *À la recherche du temps perdu*, vol. 1 (Paris: Gallimard-Pléiade, 1954), 388–89.

4. Apropos of Proust, Christian Jacob notes that no one better analyzes "the play of resonance that surrounds certain toponyms with a mysterious and evocative aura." The toponyms of the Proustian map "weave a filigree or enduring lacework between biography and psychology, and ordinary geography too, that of kilometers, latitudes, and meridians. From the spatial map we move to the map of states of mind, to the map whose places are staggered in the time of a biography, which is always a memory of lived experience. Every map is, somewhere, a Carte du Tendre by virtue of the poetic and anamnesic effects of toponymy" (*L'Empire des cartes* [Paris: Albin Michel, 1992], 304). Such is also Augé's map of the metro.

5. Norbert Lauriot notes that with the "Plan Jayot," which included prolongation of subway lines into the suburbs, the centrifugal effect of the map was "more apt to 'subjugate' the inhabitants of outer suburbs than to offer them better conditions of travel" ("La genèse d'un réseau urbain: La logique des

tracés," in *Métro-cité: Le chemin de fer métropolitain à la conquête de Paris*, ed. Sheila Hallsted-Baumert [Paris: Paris-Musées, 1997] 45). But, as Alain Cottereau insists elsewhere in the same volume, in the years 1870–1900 two urban models were considered. One was oriented toward density, in which the "polyvalence and interlace of urban activities stretched to the peripheral areas" (82). The other was "tendential," analogous to the London map, "an extension of the metropolitan region through separation of activities and zones of habitat, in the favor of suburban trains" (83).

6. Norma Evenson, in *Paris: A Century of Change, 1878–1978* (New Haven: Yale University Press, 1979), concludes her chapter on the history of the subway along the same lines: "Although public transport may become more rapid, convenient, and comfortable, the burden of a lengthy journey seems destined to remain part of the lives of many Parisians" (122). The sociohistorical treatment of degraded alienation contrasts another, of invention and ruse, by Jean-Marie Floch, in which the subway traveler is studied in the frame of a semiotic grid organized around the points of the somnambulist (passive traveler), the *arpenteur* or surveyor, the "pro" or efficient rider, and the *flâneur*, the creatively errant user of the system. His "'Etes-vous arpenteur ou somnambule?' L'élaboration d'une typologie comportementale des voyageurs du métro" (in *Sémiotique, marketing et communication: Sous les signes, les stratégies*, ed. Anne Hénault [Paris: Presses Universitaires de France, 1990], 19–27) is based in part on Augé's observations. Floch's conclusions about the ruse, wit, and tactics of subway riding are developed for the use of strategists in the line of advertisers, and market-research companies. (The translator thanks Fabienne Dumontet for calling attention to this article.)

7. A cursory review of the style and orientation of city maps in Paris from the time of Cassini (1789) until the present shows little change. Subway lines begin to appear as of 1900 and progressively resemble a skeletal system bringing forth what

might be, like the Lacanian unconscious, a "language" for Parisian space. The time-honored subway map reflects, in the words of Christian Jacob, "a rationalization in the practice of space." Aspects of the city plan are "reduced to their network, to a functional rationality, to possible circuits in an imposed system. It is up to the user to compose his or her itinerary according to criteria of what is shortest or longest, or what is logical or resides in fantasy" (*L'Empire des cartes*, 133–34).

8. The site of the subway turns to ridicule the "unconscious" that advertisers construct, or that some French critics, such as Doris-Louise Haineault and Jean-Yves Roy, have studied in *L'inconscient qu'on affiche* (Paris: Aubier, 1984), translated by Kimball Lockhart as *Unconscious for Sale: Advertising, Psychoanalysis, and the Public* (Minneapolis: University of Minnesota Press, 1993).

9. The coming of the Louvre station coincided with the going of a long-standing subway icon. Just beyond the limit of many of the stations, where ambient light illuminated the walls of the tunnels, were painted staggered signs that read "Du," then "Du Bon," and finally, "Du Bonnet," inspiring in the sequence a thirst for a spiced aperitif and the pleasure of seeing and tasting words within words. The advertisement and its technique, like the Burma-Shave panels on the American highway, are now history. In any event, city planners are increasingly using subway stops to remind travelers of a national patrimony. More and more stations are coordinating the descent into the underground with historical archaeology, especially along line 1, where are linked the Louvre, the Hôtel de Ville, and Saint-Paul. (See also Floch, "Êtes-vous arpenteur ou somnambule?" 35.)

10. The *Petit Larousse* (1974) recalls the myth with studied elegance: "A French general, born at Nantes. At Waterloo he led one of the last *carrés* of the Old Guard. There, where surrounded by a horde of enemy troops and summoned to surrender, he made the legendary statement: 'The guard is dying and does not

surrender.' According to another version, he answered with a simple word *[merde]* since known as *le mot de Cambronne.*"

11. Until Jayot's reform, the north–south line was independent of the Parisian network. The Compagnie du Nord was invested in the "suburban" plan of development that would link the *grandes lignes* to the metro. The debates about the integrity of a national system came on the heels of the Paris Commune, and thus private enterprise had to cope with the fact that on weekdays in 1901, at least ninety thousand workers went to and from the suburbs and the city. Private companies, as the 1900 Garnier map implies, offered the idea of greenery surrounding residential areas outside of Paris (Alain Cottereau, "Les batailles du métropolitain: La Compagnie du chemin de fer du Nord et les choix d'urbanisation," in Hallsted-Baumert, *Métro-cité,* 75–83).

12. Harvard Map Collection 5834 PAR 4 1911.3.

13. Lauriot, "La genèse d'un réseau urbain," 35.

14. Nicolas Papayanis, "Les transport à Paris avant le métropolitain," in Hallsted-Baumert, *Métro-cité,* 15. Material in the next two paragraphs will be drawn from this article (15–30).

15. Even if specialists of sources wonder if the work was begun in 1845–46 or in the early 1850s, the relation of the poem to the burgeoning idea of the subway cannot be discounted. Claude Pichois reviews the debates over the origins of the poem in his addenda in *Œuvres complètes de Charles Baudelaire,* vol. 1 (Paris: Gallimard-Pléiade, 1975), 839–45.

16. Lévi-Strauss's "American Indian Art in the Museum of Natural History" appeared in English in the *Gazette des Beaux-Arts* in 1945. He recasts its conclusions at the end of *La voie des masques* (Geneva: Skira, 1975).

17. Baudelaire repeatedly played on the difference. In his translation of Poe's "The Gold-Bug," when confronted with Jupiter's black idiom that affirms "I nose" (I knows), Baudelaire is impelled to add a footnote explaining that in the transliteration the reader must hear "je sens pour je sais" (I smell for I know), the nostril now a supreme site where the body meets the soul. The crossing over between English and French is taken up

in my "Colors in Translation: Baudelaire and Rimbaud," in *Rethinking Translation,* ed. Lawrence Venuti (London and New York: Routledge, 1992), 177–95.

18. And indeed it can in Augé's *Non-lieux: Introduction à une anthropologie de la surmodernité* (Paris: Seuil, 1992), 98 and 117, where he shows that the "nonplace" inhabits his verse and that for him a voyage is consummated in its invitation.

19. In *L'Écriture de l'histoire* (Paris: Gallimard, 1982), Michel de Certeau sees writing camouflaging ways of know-how, "bien vivre," or "savoir vivre" (211) that are attached to things and objects. Careful study requires "recourse to the language of gestures and tools, to those so-called tacit discourses that are made audible first of all only in the course of riots or evolutions with scythes, pitchforks, hoes, and so on. It is important to take seriously the formality of practices other than those of writing" (211–12).

20. See the illustrations (62–65) and the information summing up the discussions, about subterranean pestilence versus the destruction of the skyline that consumed Parisians and urban planners in the 1880s in Evenson, *Paris,* 91–105.

21. Ibid., 104.

22. Rabelais's story, told in *Pantagruel,* involves the trickster-hero Panurge, who sprinkles a special powder on the dress of a woman who refuses his advances. All the dogs of Paris converge on the woman and leave upon her clothing their urinary signatures. The symbolic efficacity of the narrative owes to its comic explanation of the reason why the Gobelins tapestry works, situated by the Bièvre River, smelled of ammonia being dumped into it. Readers of English and enthusiasts of the lower depths of London will find comparative matter in an epigram of Ben Jonson, "On the Famous Voyage" and "The Voyage It Selfe," in his *Poems,* ed. George Burke Johnston (Cambridge: Harvard University Press, 1955), 69–75. (The translator thanks Douglas Trevor for correlating these poems with a history of underground, city, and aroma).

23. See Nicolas Didion, "Le meilleur abri de Paris: le rôle du métropolitain au sein du programme de défense passive," in Hallsted-Baumert, *Métro-cité,* 153–62.

24. Floch notes how an irate rider reacts to being the object of study: "Ils sont marrants à la RATP! Vous savez à quoi ils perdent leur temps et notre argent? À nous étudier *in vivo,* nous les rats du métro" (They're out of their minds at the R.A.T.P.! You know how they waste their time and our money? By studying us in vivo, us, the subway rats) ("Êtes-vous arpenteur ou somnambule?" 25 n. 4).

25. Apropos of French cinema and philosophy Gilles Deleuze noted that their traditions are imbued with a passion for automata, for a Cartesianism, rid of things organic, that espouses mechanical movement. The fifth chapter of the *Discourse on Method* betrays an admiration for the human machine that percolates through films from René Clair to Jean Renoir. The *Météoré* would be the illusion [developed in Gilles Deleuze, *Cinéma 1: L'image-mouvement* (Paris: Minuit, 1983), 61–65] actualized. The Cartesian effect is putatively aimed at dispelling the experience of "the claustrophobia and clamor of subways in New York and Chicago." The designer, Bernard Kohn, admitted that "we wanted people to feel they were being welcomed to a restful and un-hectic environment" so that people could be made to "feel they are treated with dignity," as notes Craig Whitney in "Driverless Trains Have Paris Debut" (*New York Times,* October 6, 1998).

26. It might be licit to coin the term *metrocracy* to designate the peculiarity of its democracy. Lines of public and private enterprise crisscross. Early maps (such as that of 1911) take care to delineate the *ligne nord-sud* from the rest of the network (see again Cottereau, "Les batailles du métropolitain"). Subway riders cannot fail to associate the democratic feel of a train where reminders of the Third Republic linger in the station or the car. After 1970, the elimination of the first-class cars could be tied to a revival of Jacobin principles (or else the influx of foreign travelers who could not tell the difference between one type of

car and another, and were impervious to prosecution on the grounds of ignorance of the history of French aristocracy).

27. Two points are worth recalling. First, Lévi-Strauss affirmed that his *Structures élémentaires de la parenté (Elementary Structures of Kinship)* was partially inspired by the obligatory expression of an act of generosity witnessed in restaurants in southern France where workers convened at the noon hour. At the long tables it was ruled that each person had to pour the wine from the carafe at his setting into the glass of the neighbor on the opposite side. Anyone filling his own glass of wine was proscribed from the community. At the turnstile of the metro and the R.E.R. an etiquette requiring people to help their neighbor is implicit and ubiquitous. People who have misplaced their tickets and cannot exit are assisted by those who hold the doors open.

Second, in respect to the nonplace, the airport is quickly beginning to resemble the stations of an elevated global metro. The nonplace of the waiting room that Augé describes in *Non-lieux* resembles an immobile subway car. Airline companies are constructing larger nonplaces by extending the rows of business-class seats into economy cabins in accord with a strategy that increases a passenger's desire to occupy these places by obliging the client to walk through the aisle where travelers repose with peanuts and cocktails in their hands. The nonplace is more and more related to marketing.

28. Christian Jacob provides a taxinomy of deictic maps in *L'Empire des cartes,* 47–48 and 427–34.

29. Paul Éluard was said to have gone underground and to resurface, weeks later, somewhere in the New Hebrides. See Maurice Nadeau, *Histoire du surréalisme* (Paris: Gallimard, 1964).

Marc Augé, an anthropologist trained in French universities, has studied and written copiously on North African cultures. While teaching and leading seminars at École des Hautes Études en Sciences Sociales, he has authored numerous studies of contemporary culture, including *La Traversée du Luxembourg, Domaines et châteaux,* and *Non-lieux: introduction à l'anthropologie de la surmodernité.*

Tom Conley is professor of Romance languages and head of the French section at Harvard University. He is the author of *Film Hieroglyphs* and *The Self-Made Map,* and translator of Gilles Deleuze's *The Fold: Leibniz and the Baroque* and Michel de Certeau's *The Capture of Speech and Other Political Writings* and *Culture in the Plural,* all published by the University of Minnesota Press.